A
Place
Like
This

Finding Myself
In a Cape Cod Cottage

SALLY W. BUFFINGTON

Woodworth Press
La Jolla, California

Book cover and interior design by Monkey C Media
Edited by All My Best

First Edition
Printed in the United States of America

ISBN: 978-1-7371128-0-8 (Trade Paperback)
ISBN: 978-1-7371128-1-5 (eBook)

Library of Congress Control Number: 2021908415

To Andy

CONTENTS

ON HAND

*L*ate August 2011. Hurricane Irene was powering its way up the Atlantic coast, heading for New England. Three of us were on hand in this Cape Cod cottage we called Craigville: my husband Andy, his brother Pete, and I. We had all grown up with such storms and knew them "like family" in Andy's phrase, though sometimes our reminiscing sounded more like catty gossip about old classmates.

Now we had to get ready. The guys had been taught by a master, an aficionado of weather, my late mother-in-law, Lois Buffington. I could almost hear her sensible gray voice. "Now, make sure nothing's left sitting out on the lawn! Don't leave anything that the wind can take! And bring in all the furniture from the porch! Move the car into the garage! And somebody find all the lamps and candles and fill the kerosene reservoirs. Where are the flashlights and batteries? *Don't open the fridge any more than you have to!* And turn on the weather—what's Channel 4 got to say?"

I helped lift and stash things. We rushed around closing windows. I rounded up all the candles. Though we had a tightly sealed jar of matchbooks on hand, I soon learned another precaution: make sure your matches actually light. We seemed to have many that didn't.

Then what?

Wait.

Had Mom still been with us, she would have found yet more jobs. She would also have kept checking the TV or radio every few minutes; we did pretty often, too.

But she wasn't on hand and I was.

Never before had I had the chance to document the coming of a hurricane, to watch the changes personally and note the atmosphere and what it all felt like. I took off out the front door, slipping my camera in my pocket to protect it, for I knew the shutter balked when wet.

The sky was growing darker, grayer. Clouds threatened.

The yard looked as though we had never raked. Ever. Twigs and sticks lay strewn about everywhere. And all those bursts of wind! I began to wonder how any leaves still managed to cling on.

Every so often, Andy or Pete would point to a branch. "Oh, that'll probably come down!" More than once Pete said, "Well, that's how we get rid of deadwood. Don't have go up on a ladder that way."

The wind kept rising, rain grew heavier. Oak leaves glistened and raindrops shimmered at the tips of pine needles. In the woods, the normally crisp leaf layer compacted under my footsteps and turned slippery. I stood under a tree and gazed around.

No longer the usual reedy meadow with a narrow river curving through, the marsh had become a pewter-gray inland sea dashed with whitecaps. The rain-stippled surface looked like fabric with a lot of snags. On it, a flotilla of ducks and Canada geese bobbed about as though enjoying a church social.

Back in the yard once more, I found my umbrella kept blowing inside out. I wanted to shout to the roaring wind, "Hallelujah! You go, sister! Amen, brother!"

Time to get indoors.

It was 2 p.m. The power failed. With its deep surrounding overhang of porches, the cottage interior soon got dark. I had hauled out anything which would hold a votive, taper, or pillar: small plates and little bowls, as well as Mom's tall turquoise glass dolphin candlesticks, elegant Metropolitan Museum reproductions. Most of them, I'd clumped in the middle of the dining table, with an island outpost on the coffee table in the living room.

Toward evening, all those candles and the red tablecloth transformed the setup into a virtual campfire. As we gathered 'round for supper, the wind kept scouring about and throwing noisy gusts at the windows. Though I had set out cheese, sliced meat, wine, and fruit, I realized I had forgotten bread. "Sorry, guys. Anything else you want while I'm getting stuff from the fridge?"

"Nope, but be quick, we gotta preserve any cold we can." For just a moment, Andy's warning tone brought Mom back.

When I sat down once more, he said, "Here's to the cottage!"

At "Cheers!" from Pete, we all clinked glasses and dug into our indoor picnic. The candlelight made the raised decoration on the old china plates look like embossed silver; with a single flame behind it, my pinot noir appeared portentous, even a bit infernal. No elegance for us three, though; as the temperature had fallen, we had all bundled up in layers of sweaters and old sweatshirts.

Andy leaned back in his chair, eyes glinting, and asked Pete, "Remember the '44 Hurricane?"

"Oh, yeah, that one destroyed the beach houses completely." Pete took a sip of wine. "We were kids then, but I sure remember it! And it hit this village hard—took down the steeple on the Tabernacle, didn't it? And a whole lot of trees and branches!"

The guys chewed over that storm awhile; then I brought up Hurricane Carol, the first one that had registered in my life, mainly by sending a huge tree down across my street. I was six then, and that fallen tree constitutes my entire memory. Next we turned to Hurricane Bob, back in August 1991. During that one, I had been staying with my mother elsewhere on Cape Cod and was scheduled to fly out the next day to get our kids back to California for the start of school. Our usual snooze of a bus trip to Boston's Logan Airport took on an aspect of Pony Express desperation.

Flying out, however, had meant leaving Pete and Mom behind at the cottage to cope with recovery. Pete snorted, "Oh, you got off easy! We didn't have power for a week! It was downright rugged around here." I suppose I did sort of cheat that time, though with no such intent.

And on and on we went, remembering Carol, Bob, Diane, and all the other hurricanes we had known.

At 8 p.m., the brothers turned in. Irene had died down some, but pitch dark surrounded us. Not yet tired, I settled back down at the table. *Oh, rats! All these candles—but they sure don't make for much light to read by.* I kept on trying anyway. Around my flickery little outpost, the dark felt almost furry and somehow the house seemed to have taken on an extending series of rooms. Yet when I went in search of another sweater, I felt like a small animal trying to navigate a dense thicket. With only a single candle, it sure helped that I already knew where I was going. *Did all the flashlights get taken upstairs?*

Should anyone have been crazy enough to be out that night, she or he might have looked up at our window and seen my face. Reading at my table of light—though other people and houses surrounded us—I might as well have been afloat at sea. Wrapped in wind in my dining room "cabin," I felt like the captain of the cottage ship: a lone figure amid the darkness.

By the time of Hurricane Irene, I had been going to the cottage for more than forty summers. I had also gone to Cape Cod itself from infancy, vacationed with my family, and lived there full time in my teenage years. Tonight, however, was my first time as the woman on hand in a storm.

Long before I had married in, my practical, no-nonsense mother-in-law had often weathered such storms; she had also set in place many family practices and domestic customs. But now the cottage and the people in it—and the soul of the place—lived with, not under, a different kind of domestic leader, a less commanding and more collaborative one. While Mom had been a manager *par excellence*, I generally assumed that the people around me would figure out what needed to be done and spent my time living a creative life as well as keeping the place running.

She and I both loved the cottage, yet I had taken time to breathe in the place, to nurture its history and happiness. Not only had I gone tramping out in the woods and photographed leaves and rising water that afternoon, but later I would also write an account of the storm and what we had gone through.

But I had not always felt free to operate that way.

Over the years, my stays at Craigville had weathered me, even as they offered that great place of Cape Cod welcome and respite. First passing through stages of naïve newness, I had struggled to define myself. At times I'd felt like a figurehead—Cottage Daughter-In-Law—rather than a woman in command of herself. The family had met me with both affection and head winds, later a kind of useful opposition—and once a personal storm that rocked me profoundly.

The next morning, Irene having departed, the power was back on and so was the sun! The view looked as though it had had its face washed. Out in the marsh, the tide had receded, and the scene was painted in crayon colors: sky blue, yellow-green reeds, chocolate brown mud. Except for the braying of chainsaws, the air was quiet again. No more roaring wind.

Though hundreds of fallen twigs and pinecones remained for us to rake up, the cottage had sustained only minor wounds: a ripped porch screen and a branch lying across the path down by the road. The tree looked as though an arm had been wrenched from its socket, the shreds of sapwood like torn tendons.

The cottage had made it through—and so had I.

MEETING THE HOUSE

"Now we've got to go to Craigville!"

January 28, 1968. We'd been engaged barely twenty-four hours when my fiancé, Andy Buffington, proposed this; I had thought we were simply on our way back to Boston after the weekend with my parents in Brewster, on Cape Cod. Andy had told me about Craigville, but I hadn't expected to meet the place so soon. Now I realized that it, too, was an honored and vital member of the family.

What Andy called Craigville (about twenty miles from Brewster) turned out to be a big, old weathered-shingle house planted on a hillside, surrounded by other dowager summer cottages. The place was shut up for winter in what I would learn was typical Buffington fashion: thorough, careful work had been done. With all the furnishings covered in old sheets, the water and power shut off, and the screens and curtains taken down, the place slumbered in a degree of induced desolation that verged on comical. A discolored slab of plywood protected the front door; bare branches, swirling dry leaves, and bleached-out grass added to the forlorn impression.

However stripped and wintery it looked, I saw the cottage with summer eyes. I was high as a kite and in love! So was Andy. Also, I had lived on Cape Cod year 'round; I knew the transforming magic summer would bring. Though I shivered when we stepped into the cottage and the dank air seemed as cold as the water of baptism must feel to an infant, I was undaunted. That whole weekend had been full of contrast and transformation.

The day before, Andy had proposed to me in brilliant sun on First Encounter Beach in Eastham, which he had chosen because he knew I loved the place. But as the result of a lengthy cold snap, everything was frozen. What water we could see was a deep Prussian blue; over much of the beach, wind had sculpted sea foam into mini-icebergs that looked like meringues. Sitting next to me on one, Andy said, "Will you go to California with me?"

Given our situation together, I knew he meant "Will you marry me?"

Of course, I said "Yes!" Which came to mean, for over fifty years ago now, that California has been our permanent home. Every summer we have flown Pacific to Atlantic—always to Cape Cod—and then Atlantic to Pacific back again, migrating birds in a bicoastal life.

Summers at the cottage, though I knew and admired Andy's calm, dignified father, I soon recognized his mother was in charge. Vigorous, articulate, and attractive, Mom was the center of it all. My "Can I help?" requests translated into such things as bed making, dishwasher loading, salad assembly, and vacuuming. But real maintenance and labor, the upkeep of the cottage over time, devolved on Mom and Dad—and for the seventeen years after he died, on her alone.

Summer after summer, though, the cottage worked on me, this big old wooden ark of a place with its hospitable porches and dining room table that could seat twelve. Memories soon piled up, including assorted birthday celebrations, Mom and Dad's fiftieth anniversary, the family's kind response the summer I broke my leg, and our niece's wedding. I kept remembering conversations out on the cool porch, all the old Laurel and Hardy, Mickey Mouse, and family movies shown on the noisy old projector, snapshots taken on the front steps and all the family stories I learned there—and the house's own creation story.

In 1906, Annie Fisher, a local businesswoman and Andy's father's great aunt, laid claim to a "dance pavilion" (or hall) no longer being used in a hotel nearby. Sensing an opportunity, Aunt Annie (as I always heard her called) hired workmen to put this room on logs and roll it to the summit of a small hillside on Ocean Avenue. They divided the dance hall into living- and dining room, then added a kitchen, bathroom, and porch. The living room featured a fireplace and chimney and extended into a further downstairs room. A flight of stairs led up to the second story: five bedrooms and bath radiating out from a small platform-like hallway. Outside, Aunt Annie had a partial wraparound porch built, as well as a walkway up to the front door, which faced the marsh and Centerville River rather than Ocean Avenue.

In 1938, Andy's parents bought the place from her; they added a foundation and basement under the kitchen and downstairs bedroom, and later a much-needed extra bathroom. When Andy got into photography as a teen, part of the maid's room (off the kitchen) became his darkroom; later it got turned into a pantry. Best of all, the section of porch outside the living room was screened in, creating a space we have all loved so much that my sister-in-law once said, "Well, you can sell the house, but keep the porch!"

In spite of this somewhat accidental architecture, what emerged was a remarkable house. Still quirky and a bit old fashioned, Craigville is today a fortuitous mix of indoors and out, airy treehouse and solid old family cottage. And over the years, some unknown wizard has kept waving a magic wand over the house, leaving behind an invisible trail of enjoyment like an extended bubble. All this from what was essentially a salvage operation.

Aunt Annie christened the place "Hillcrest," but the title did not last. Like many other families before and since, instead we have appropriated the name of the village where the cottage is located, as though ours were the only structure there that mattered. I soon fell in with the family custom of calling the cottage "Craigville."

Such a name is more than a little presumptuous, but something important gets conveyed. Naming a place and remembering it, telling stories about the raccoons that came down the chimney or arguing over when the roof was repaired or where we bought the new dishwasher or how we weathered a hurricane: all these things make houses grow into more than boxes to live in. Houses almost become people who figure in the landscapes of our hearts and minds.

And when I use the family name for this Buffington cottage in the village of Craigville on Cape Cod, it means that I, too, have moved in. I am part of this place, part of Craigville: a compound of house and family, people and land. Craigville has played a role in my life I will never stop dealing with. Like a complex parent whose rooms and customs and history stand in for personal qualities, the cottage has nurtured and brought me up. In spite of its vocal male denizens, I think of Craigville as female; one of my first personifications was calling it a "mother hen." I have also termed the cottage an "ark," alluding to Noah. In its gather-us-all-together way, the cottage is and has been a mother to me, to us all, and a constant in our lives. A village-worth of happenings is contained in the place. Only a collective word does it justice.

Why just "village?" Why not "city" or "country?" Not only do those terms seem over-grand, but also the small-place specificity is important. No large or influential organism on earth, this family is sufficient unto itself. While we have never gone so far as to call the cottage "Buffington-ville," in it we have created and engaged in a lot of our own customs and as sometimes happens, acted as a closed-minded little society in which an outsider has a hard time. Yet as I well know, this outsider can be molded as well as nurtured by the village—and come to love it.

So Craigville it is. And in using this village name, I mean the Buffington family house and the surrounding land its creator called "Hillcrest."

Just about every day of my life, I return in mind to Craigville. That is, to many visions of that sprawling old house. In my favorite one, it is always summer, expansive and comfortable, sunlit and warm. Always the porch awaits me, open and hospitable. Sun dapples the lawn. Birds fly about in the branches, the dishwasher roars in the kitchen, full from breakfast and supper the night before; beds are made, the day ahead planned, and I sit down to write, pen poised to take charge of paper. Sun streams in on the surface of the desk and, as the trees stir lightly outside, their branches extend toward me, all the while spreading lattices of shadows on the ground beneath.

WHO WAS I?

Betrothal Revealed.

Oh, that heading! It should have been printed in heliotrope or mauve, in some florid Gothic typeface, reflecting the romance novel phrasing used by the *Cape Cod Standard-Times* to announce my engagement to Andy. We all snickered over it for weeks.

The product of training by three parents, I was well-schooled in politeness, though not the announcement's prissy style. I speak of three parents because my gentle English grandmother, Sallie Braithwaite, lived with or near us throughout my growing-up years. I was also accustomed to being listened to and taken seriously. In many late-night discussions, my beloved father had taught me to think for myself; he had also instilled in me the idea that finding my path in life and then pursuing it was all important.

By the time I met Andy, without realizing it, I thought of myself as unique, a sense that came of being an only child, playing the flute as though the instrument itself were an identity—and most of all, feeling that no one else regarded the world quite the way I did.

I had always assumed I would get married sooner or later; however, I had never considered planning a wedding or choosing china and silver patterns—let alone thought about what marriage was like, or dealing with in-laws, having children, or what we would do in the summers. Instead, once Andy and I had set our June wedding date, my worry was, *With all this going on, how can I manage to practice enough to pull off my senior recital?*

For I was nearing the end of four years at the New England Conservatory of Music, and my senior recital that March was the crowning event of my training; it was the occasion on which I would prove I was ready to step out and be publicly known as a flutist.

I should have instead given an eloquent speech on how I loved music itself. Classical music was then a faith and a religion to me, something to breathe in with all my senses, far beyond the air which I used to play the flute. I had gone to the conservatory for the love of music, with no practical sense of how life would play out afterward.

Thus, I had spent four years of heaven in a crazy cloister, punch drunk on music among other benign drunks. When we were not in class or practicing or studying theory or harmony or music history or counterpoint, my friends and I bought and compared LPs (long-playing records), listened to the Metropolitan Opera every Saturday afternoon, or went to free concerts. We might as well have eaten music, the way we consumed it, all the while talking over endless ice cream at Brigham's or crummy meals in the dorm cafeteria. To cover everyday expenses, I ushered at concerts, a job I regarded as being paid to hear music; during my last two years, I worked part time at a wholesale music company. So absorbed was I, the Sixties hardly touched me.

The bedrock underneath all this was several hours a day of solitary work in little cells called practice rooms; one evening when the conservatory building was crowded, I even used a broom closet. All I needed was my flute, a stand, and sheet music. Not only did this train me in discipline—there was no such thing as "musician's block"—it also reinforced self-reliance and at its grandest, the sense of working at my own destiny. Yet I was self-made only to a degree: the bedrock under the bedrock was weekly lessons with my master teacher, James Pappoutsakis of the Boston Symphony Orchestra.

However, in that conservatory world, I was unusual in that I still read avidly, and I think I was the only person in the dorm who read *Time* magazine or any other news. I also kept a very occasional journal; life felt so amazing that I had to try to hold onto it.

Planning for our wedding (my mother did most of the work) and getting ready to move to California, I went through the motions of normal life—if "going through the motions" can be applied to someone doing everything as sincerely and eagerly as I did. What lay beyond? I might as well have been about to step off the edge of a square world. I just kept finding out as I went along. As for future family relationships, or how Craigville would come to figure in my life, I barely thought about them. I was in love with Andy and life spread before us.

However, I had already gotten clues that I was about to participate in a different kind of family life. Instead of the quiet atmosphere in which I had been brought up to listen as well as politely keep up my end of the conversation, I met a major "hammer and tongs" style of talk.

At the Buffington home, navigating the conversation meant struggling to insert a word. Andy's mother (Mom) was so different from my own mother; she led the pack at family dinners. As though competing with the clinks and chinks of cutlery on plates, everyone except Mr. Buffington and I held forth. Quips, family stories, opinions, silliness, and leaps of nothing-resembling-logic—all galloped along. Mom proudly had a term for it: "twig to twig," which meant changes of subject at whim. You had to be quick indeed to follow, let alone participate. Whether at home in their year-round house in southeastern Massachusetts, or the week before our wedding at the cottage, every Buffington dinner felt like a party to me, and a competitive one at that.

Over the years that followed, I would keep finding this impression accurate, especially at Craigville. Though I became another Mrs. Buffington, in some ways I remained Sally Woodworth, an "only" in the hubbub, quietly holding on as I kept up with the flow. I marveled at the Buffingtons' cheer and informational quickness; this was a bright, educated bunch of people. At the same time, I was often driven inward and continued to think independently: to be my own person.

I was also reckoning with the cottage itself. Ironically, holding open the front door on a breezy day stood an old cast iron doorstop that presented a visual definition of the classic Cape Cod cottage: peaked-roof, center chimney, white clapboard walls, and "six over six" paned windows. Pink, yellow, and red roses draped decoratively over the front of the house while a flagstone path led up to the door bisecting a perfect green lawn. A vision we've all seen: think of the covers of novels, chamber of commerce brochures, postcards, housing developments—and even a tapestry on a friend's California living room wall.

A vison which is just what Craigville is not.

However, a cottage like the doorstop one, though absent much romance, appealed to my parents and particularly my mother, whose outlook on life was rather English: what you needed in a house was efficient comfort and lack of fuss, quietly attractive décor, and, as she put it, "Not a lot to keep up." As a young child, just about every summer I had been taken on two-week vacations with my parents to Cape Cod cottages in various towns; later we owned a cottage colony called Nauset Haven in Eastham, where we rented out nine such cottages to families like ours. After later selling the cottage business, my parents bought a year-round "Cape," a neat little box in the town of Brewster.

By contrast, while hardly a mansion on the scale of Chatham or Osterville (wealthy Cape Cod summer communities), our Craigville constituted something of a law unto itself. As you walked around it, you got little or no clue to what shape or architectural style you would meet on the side ahead. Also, rather than the "light housekeeping" cottages my family advertised for rent, Craigville was a summer house encompassing a year's worth of lifestyle, complex and detailed.

And then I had other ideas about Cape Cod houses. Often in my teen years, my father would say something like, "You want to come with me and see a new house, Sal? I've got to get a For Sale photo for the office ad this week." Climbing into his truck, we would take off together and soon get to talking about what we were seeing.

"You notice how nicely these Cape houses fit in, Sal?" Cigarette holder in hand, Daddy would gesture out the window. "I like the way they settle into the land, don't you?"

"Yeah, and they're pretty, too. I like this one with the soft green shutters!"

"But that pink-shutter job next door looks just prissy. They're not supposed to be 'cute'—the thing about these houses is they're plain and comfortable." He tapped some cigarette ash into the pull-out tray.

"How about that one over there with the dark green shutters?"

"Uh-huh, that's handsome; oh, and this dark blue's a good trim color, too, very classic . . . . Now, what d'ya think of this one?" He slowed down and we inspected a Cape-type house somehow melded with a split level whose shutters and front and garage doors were all painted brilliant orange.

"Ugh."

"Yeah, that one's just too gussied up. The whole thing is, they aren't supposed to be big suburban-type places; they're down-to-earth houses for families. You know, maybe later the owners added a little color for trim, but basically they stuck with building clean, nice places."

"I do like them better with shutters, though, Daddy. They look so bare without." We were passing a frown of a house with no plants or shrubs, let alone shutters.

"Yup, you've got that right, Sal. But the main thing is, these old Cape houses are classic designs—and some of the modern versions are, too. Even a couple of hundred years out, they're still attractive. They work for people."

I was being quietly schooled in a way of thinking about the world: build what you need, keep it nicely, and don't get pretentious. In the process, you might create a classic.

Another kind of Cape Cod house I heard about resided in books; first and foremost, *The Outermost House* by Henry Beston. My parents gave copies to their friends and family. I remember my father saying to his favorite aunt when she visited from California, "Dorothy, this is the real thing. This guy really experienced it, the spirit of the land, the Great Beach . . . ." He spoke as though Beston's book was sacred writing about a sacred place. A gospel of living in nature, it is a poetic account of the Thoreau-like year of 1926 which Beston spent living alone on the Outer Beach in Eastham. Heated by a small wood stove, his two-room shack (sixteen by twenty feet) was a toehold of a house located way, way out in the dunes.

Another: *The House on Nauset Marsh*, by Wyman Richardson. Like Beston's, it was located in Eastham, the town where we lived. Writing of birding, fishing, and hunting in the glorious marsh surrounding his house, Richardson wrote less poetically than Beston, yet both men's words conveyed intensity and a personal view. Though their house was less exposed to the elements, clearly Richardson and his family regarded their house as a haven away from society—again, a place in nature.

As for Thoreau, his book *Cape Cod* lived in our bookcase next to *Walden*, though I read neither book until many years later. However, in those teen years, I had already responded to a line from *Cape Cod*: "A man may stand there and put all America behind him."

A ringing declaration! The independent soul stepped forth, as though having digested America, and stood ready to forge ahead solo—on the great Atlantic outer beach at that, so close to where I lived. I had walked there myself.

How did I know these words? In 1962, when I was sixteen, the Cape Cod National Seashore was signed into being by President Kennedy, a creation which was a huge local issue. My parents and I listened to heated debates, attended meetings, and watched as signage, trails, and new roads got put in, as well as the handsome visitor center within walking distance of us. The Seashore used this quote from Thoreau in much of its printed material.

All these words and books planted in me the sense that on Cape Cod, I was living on holy ground. What was more, I might even come to know its essence: Cape Cod as a refuge in nature, a place of the soul. You might venture out from your house, itself modest and all you needed to survive, but your real need—your heart's home—was the wild, open, natural world. Yet people built houses and summer homes there and moved upon this holy ground. What you built and how you lived mattered.

Still another book about Cape Cod had opened quite a different door. To pique my mother's and my interest before we moved there, my father read aloud Joseph Lincoln's *Mr. Pratt,* a novel from 1920. While *Mr. Pratt* was hardly great literature, Daddy chose especially well for his younger listener; every chapter ended on a cliff-hanger, and Lincoln included a lot of funny incidents.

The protagonist, Mr. Pratt, is a wise old Cape Cod salt who meets up with two rich young New Yorkers who have read *The Simple Life* (a highly influential bestseller in its day) and come in search of "the natural life." Pratt, of course, is skeptical yet intrigued, though he comes to know and like the naïve young men as he guides them through a series of adventures. To them, "the natural life" means living without creature comforts—the more primitive things get, the better—and putting the business world behind. Mr. Pratt, of course, thinks they are crazy. He's been "livin' the natr'l life all his life!" Needless to say, the New Yorkers do not succeed and get a bit shaken up in the process;

eventually they find their true loves and rush right back to their New York society lives.

Not only was this very human story associated with Cape Cod, but via Mr. Pratt, Lincoln made much of the contrast between locals and summer people in big, fancy places: the "wash-ashores" vs. the natives. And as it turned out, I myself was about to become, not a "real" Cape Codder (born there), but someone who lived there. A local, at least for seven years.

Whenever I went to Craigville, though, I felt as though I had gone over to the "other side," where I visited a big family summer house surrounded by other big fancy houses, swam at a private beach, and learned the established social customs of that quaint seasonal community to which the Buffingtons belonged.

Though my father visited Craigville only occasionally, he was with me in spirit all the time, present in his independent, skeptical-of-established-families stance, born of his own in-law experiences. His comment on one of his own family members was typical. "I sometimes wonder if he's all that bright, Sal . . . ." I was his daughter in this way as well as in the love of reading, research on beloved topics, and independent investigation indoors and out. Still a Californian at heart after decades on the east coast, Daddy possessed a westerner's "strike out for yourself" frame of mind. Impatient with speculation or thoughts of the moment, he also expected himself and others to know whereof they spoke and why they thought what they did.

During my teen years, one of Daddy's and my favorite excursions was to walk the flats. On the west side of the outer Cape, on Cape Cod Bay, beaches go from full swimming depth at high tide to spread-out expanses of horizontal, almost dry sand at dead low tide, six hours later. Two such cycles per day. Whenever you go, you are in the midst of vast change, albeit gradual. Before your eyes, flat sand dries from tan to white in the sun or disappears under rippling wavelets. Or you stand in a tiny bay as it merges into rising water, while junior waves flow; or sand washes away from under your feet as the tide pulls out; or an incoming current treats you as an island to surround—or surmount, even carry off, if you are not careful on some beaches.

At dead low, the flats are transcendent. You walk and walk in and out of inch-deep pools, across expanses of sand in all stages of wet or dry or in between. Except for the occasional plane or bird call, quiet reigns. People's figures are transformed by distance into walking clothespins. You walk and walk . . . deeper water is out there. Somewhere.

"Look at all those holes, Sal!" Daddy might spot a cluster of nail-head sized pits near a few blades of beach grass.

"You want to dig some clams?"

"Nope! Let 'em be."

Or we would wave to people we saw and fling out, "Nice day!"

We always picked up scallop shells, something neither of us could resist. "We've only got a few hundred of these at home, you know."

Space. Sky, sand, water, sun, clouds, salt air. Wind. At some point, though, we would have to turn back. Tides turn and all that space can deceive, and it was a long way back to where we had started from.

So just what would Sally Woodworth make of Craigville? This tight, little community and its crowded beach with little or no difference between high and low tide? How would she sustain a quiet inner life in this arena? Where might she find quiet outdoor beauty?

Further, not only was Craigville village full of commodious old family houses, but also, how would this independent soul make her way in the buzzing hive of bees that was the Buffington house, this place they called "the cottage?"

MY NEW FAMILY

*H*ere is the Buffington family in 1967, the summer before I married Andy. Standing in the front yard, with the cottage behind them, are Dad and his sons. Jim is the eldest, in the red shirt; Pete stands on the right-hand end, and Andy, the youngest, on the left. Seated, my soon-to-be mother-in-law and sister-in-law anchor the ends of the bench, Mom on the left, Judy on the right. Jim and Judy's kids, Jon, Joanna (later known as Jo), and Jimmy (ages six, nine, and ten), squeeze in between. So crowded together are the three generations, I might well have wondered, *Is there room for me?*

Mom (Lois Buffington) looks proud and happy, while Dad (James Buffington Jr.) presents an "old man of the mountains" visage though, as always, his expression is calm and benign. As for his sons, Andy and Pete in white shirts appear to declare, "We're the young professionals." Oddly, "Jim Three" (as Andy's older brother was sometimes called) and his son, "young Jimmy," contribute a touch of goofiness, even insouciance. With the only dark expression, my sister-in-law Judy looks as though she would rather be anywhere else but here, though perhaps this could be attributed to a hot day and unwilling kids ("How long do I gotta sit here?")—or was it a pervasive unease?

Life at the cottage was summer camp for all ages, with Mom as director. Kids had activities: tennis, swimming lessons, chores. Adults had the house: paint to scrape and prime and renew, lawns to mow, food to shop for, then The Beach; later, drinks on the porch, dinner, and Talk.

I soon decided that Andy was the most individual of the three sons. On meeting (we were introduced by mutual friends), I was both charmed and puzzled by his mix of cheerfulness, originality, intelligence, and a soaring confidence that carried him along like a speedboat. Mixing physics jargon (of which I knew nothing) into ordinary conversation, Andy talked and acted as though life should run on a mix of scientific principles and down-home Buffington wisdom, all this with immense enthusiasm and flashes from his very blue eyes. Handsome and full of energy and terrible puns, he seemed utterly quirky—and was of a very different world from mine (or much of anybody else's for that matter), high energy physics research at MIT.

I had not taken even high school physics, so more than just his jargon was off-putting when I first visited "the lab." Everyone there was friendly, though surrounded by towering stacks of computer printouts and banks of clunky equipment jammed with wires and electronics. The humming, room-sized IBM 360 they all used was the first computer I had ever seen. Thrown though I was, I think I dimly sensed a commonality: these people engaged in long hours of private work on pursuits hardly known to the outside world, much as musicians also did. (We, however, needed far less voluminous equipment.)

Once I got introduced to these guys and other friends of Andy's, I found that many of them, like him, played music, often impressively well; they loved to talk about it, too. Andy had played the piano since the age of five and was also interested in the harpsichord.

Yet at the cottage, Andy merged right back into the family and again became one of the Buffington boys, the group I would later call The Broze. Right from the start, I noticed that Jim and Andy loved to twit Pete, the boy-in-the-middle, as they had done when they were kids. In photos, Jim often assumed a gleeful, slitty-eyed look and was prone to poking up rabbit-ear fingers behind Pete's head.

Jim also liked to catch my eye, elbow Andy in the ribs, and in a tone of mixed ridicule and pride toss out, "'Uterly wet and a weed' . . . but he's my bro!" Or he would say of Andy, "He's all wet and a weed," followed by "Hee, hee!" Then Jim would turn to me, grinning and chortling, with a gleeful expression that said, "I'm the one on top."

We might be carrying dishes out to the kitchen after dinner when Andy would say, "Hey Presto, pots and pans!" If I made references to manners, I might be greeted with "Politeness be jumbled and bumbled and banged!"

What was all this about?

This family did not have a *lingua franca*, it had a *lingua biblia*. Those refrains and quotes, I soon learned, came from two beloved books about—guess what?—groups of juvenile males. "Uterly wet and a weed" [sic] is from *Down with Skool* by Geoffrey Willans and Ronald Searle, an idiosyncratic, hilarious look at the British boys' "public" school system. "Hey Presto, pots and pans" leaps from the pages of *The Magic Pudding*, an Australian children's classic from 1918, a huge hit with the Buffington boys. Of course, the statement, "Politeness be jumbled and bumbled and banged!" would appeal to many kids, not just these three. Another apt quote was "bounding and plunging," which it seemed to me the Buffingtons did verbally all the time; they took pride in it, too.

As for the pudding, it was a "cut and come again" pot on two spindly legs that got carried about and offered a wide choice of favorite foods, slice after slice. Although a grumpy, spiteful complainer, the pudding never ran out of whatever you wanted—and thus the possession of it was worth endless fighting and scheming over. The three good guys (the brothers, of course) owned the Puddin'; the bad guys, the Possum and the Wombat, were "snooting, snouting," devious creatures. In an incident from early in the book, one of the good guys says, "We shall have to fight them, as usual."

'Why do you have to fight them?' asks another.

'Because they're after our Puddin.'"

The Buffington boys did not go out and fight—they talked. And the ever-renewing character of the pudding, plus all the bumptious talk and behavior, expressed the family character well. The boys had complete faith in themselves, as well as a proud, protective defensiveness. And why not?

Unlike the Buffington boys, however, those Australian bush characters were uneducated. All three brothers had suffered through Phillips Exeter Academy ("Phillips Exzcema," in Andy's schoolboy reference), and later graduated from fine colleges (Harvard, MIT, and Columbia Business School). Probably Willans and Searle's British public "skool" had much in common with Exeter: boys together, school food, pranks, and horsing around. From the Broze' stories I heard, plenty of one-upmanship went on, and a lot of classifying other kids as "uterly wet and a weed"—or however the Exeter parlance of the 1950s had it.

As for my new mother- and father-in-law, Mom and Dad (I only came to call her "Mom" after a few years), they were friendly indeed and tickled pink to break out the champagne the night Andy and I visited when newly engaged. In their eyes, Andy had taken a long time to get married (he was twenty-nine to my twenty-two), and I have been told that I was far more approved of than several of his former girlfriends.

Much like my parents, Mr. and Mrs. Buffington were comfortable middle-class people and Protestant; also, all four of our parents were about the same age and liked each other immediately. When we found pieces of the same silver pattern in both families, everyone took it as an omen that Andy and I were fated to be happy together.

However, the Buffingtons welcomed me so cordially that I failed to appreciate one warning about possible family challenges I was given, though I never quite forgot it.

Ten days after our wedding, Andy and I flew to Berkeley and took up residence in California. One evening a few months later, we were invited to dinner at the home of one of his colleagues, along with another colleague and family. Both families lived in the rapidly developing East Bay suburbs, both had four children, and both wives, Joyce and Sue, personified suburban motherhood. Their "kinder, kuche, kirche" lives were probably little different from how Mom and my mother had lived.

As for me, I was trying to figure out a heady combo of married life, California (and what felt like several separate worlds within it), my flute career, and finding a graduate school. I did not plan on having children for some time, either, so was on the pill.

While we chatted over the dishes after supper (the guys were off discussing physics in the living room), Joyce asked how I liked Andy's mother. I replied that I did not know her well yet, although Mom had been welcoming and friendly.

"Oh, just you wait! It always feels easy at first. Later on, you'll find mothers-in-law are tough!" Sue said grimly.

They turned to me. "Gee, I think Andy's mother is a lot of fun! I like her."

"You'll find out!" Grim, sure tones of voice. Both nodded fervently. *What a cliché*, I thought. *"I can't get along with my mother-in-law!" Sounds like something out of a comic book or a soap opera.*

Though I went on chatting politely, I told myself, *You don't have to think that way, Sally. You can do better. It won't be like that for you.*

From then on, every summer Andy and I flew to Cape Cod for several weeks, staying equal time with each family. At the cottage, I would help out, fit in as best I could, and keep trying to read the family geography. In those early years, my sister-in-law Judy was usually there with her three kids, and both my brothers-in-law came down on weekends. "Mom and Dad's room" was the only bedroom downstairs, off the living room. Something of a sandwich room with the basement below and two bedrooms above, it was almost at the center of the house.

In time, I would come to think of the whole cottage as Mom's room. The place was entwined with her, much as in the scene James Thurber depicted in *House and Woman*. There, the woman's head and upper torso form the entire back wall and her upper arm morphs into the roof. Though that cartoon implies a male-female relationship rather than mother-family, Mom came to embody the cottage for me, too. Investing herself via activity enough for two managers, she encompassed the entire outfit.

FITTING IN

*E*venings at Craigville, eight or ten of us would take our places around the dining table under the Victorian hanging lamp. The menu might feature swordfish, corn on the cob, often a pork roast on the weekend, and finish off with blueberry pie or ice cream for dessert. All cooked beautifully by Mom, though Judy and I did our best to help out in the kitchen. Always wine in the handsome old glasses—and so much laughing, it was like champagne bubbling. Everyone together being Buffingtons, telling stories and jokes, going over the day.

At 6:25, however, this all came to a dead halt. Mom would turn on the TV by the sideboard. "Quiet, everyone! Time for the weather!" Voices would trail off in mid-sentence. "Remember the night we . . ." "I was talking to . . ."

"Do we *have to?*"

"Shhh!" Mom would say sharply. "Listen!"

The lesson had begun. "Here's Don Kent, WBZ TV Weatherbee, with the evening weather report!" We were back in the classroom and our teacher was a dark-haired man, with a Boston accent and beetling eyebrows, who stood talking in front of a blackboard covered with the cabalistic symbols of weather forecasting. "Weather conditions are mostly cloudy skies with highs in the upper seventies."

One of the kids might ask, "Can I have the salt?"

"Shhh!" Her nose and forehead wrinkled in irritation, Mom would bend toward him or her. Someone would furtively pass the salt.

"For tomorrow, the forecast is scattered showers in the morning, winds south-southeast at ten miles an hour. It'll be muggy, humidity seventy-five percent, with partial clearing throughout the afternoon." As he spoke, Mr. Kent gestured and pointed to curved weather front lines with their pennants of white triangles, all the while reciting temperatures across New England. His arms roamed the chalked map.

Hardly daring to lift a fork, we all sat stock still. During the commercial, Judy might say to Mom, "Shall I get the ice cream out to soften a bit now?"

"Yes, but be quiet, he's coming back on now, and I want to know what tomorrow will be!"

Finally, he signed off. "This is Don Kent, WBZ Channel 4, Boston. Good night!"

We could speak again. We had weathered the weather report.

I, too, had grown up in Massachusetts, but in my family, weather was something just quietly dealt with. Not so at Craigville, where it seemed that the sun magnetically drew laundry out of the washing machine onto the clothesline. Early. (Mom sometimes called up the stairs for dirty clothes before we were out of bed.) At the end of the machine's cycle, I could almost visualize the shirts and sheets taking off for outdoors, where clothespins quivering with eagerness waited to clip them down. Paint got slapped on to dry fast, lawns got mowed before the mercury rose. On my very first visit, I was introduced to the Brisker, a piece of apparently standard kitchen equipment: a box with a low-level heater to combat softening crackers and potato chips.

Though I stayed at Craigville only a week or two at a time, being there was total immersion. I often felt like one of British novelist Barbara Pym's characters going home at Christmas. ". . . people seemed to lose their status as individuals in their own right and became diminished in stature, mere units in families, when for the rest of the year they were bold and original . . . ." My California life seemed like an existence on another planet.

The opposite of "diminished," Mom was a compact woman with gray eyes and a wonderful smile who never questioned that she was in charge. While she would sometimes ask Dad, "What do you think, Jim?" Mom ran everyday life.

A fine cook, she avidly read both the recipes and descriptive books in her *Time-Life Foods of the World*. Their looks at culture and place followed on the many foreign trips she and Dad took, which Mom photographed intensively with her prized Leica. She also read much nonfiction and history, avidly read *The New Yorker*, and especially admired the writing of John McPhee. Politically, Mom was a Republican and utterly distrusted "the Dems." She was also a saver of useful things like index cards for "unregistered person" (from a long-ago campaign) whose backs she used for recipes.

All together, she embraced her role as CDO: Chief Domestic Officer. One summer, I told Mom how Andy felt I had been bossing him and our kids around too much; he and I had argued over this shortly before flying east. She answered, "Someone's got to be in charge, to keep the whole outfit going. You're doing the right thing!"

Although cottage customs and expectations were not formally expressed, rules were clear; I did my best to fit in. Do not sleep late, breakfast is at 7:30. For everyone. Eat what is served to you, like it or not. Make your kids eat it, too. Every bit of it, down to the last crumb. This table is "the Clean Plate Club." Do not bother watching the sunset or linger to talk after dinner; it is time to do the dishes. Pitch in. Now. Bread is always served in the African wood trough, gin and tonic in the tall green-leaf glasses. Reuse your paper napkin until it becomes as fragile as lace. Never put clothes in the dryer, we have a clothesline. Work around the yard. Do not walk to the beach in your bathing suit.

During my first few summer stays, Mom, Judy, and I would go on a special excursion to the Sail Loft, a women's specialty store nearby, where a Craigville acquaintance, Mrs. Jack (not Jackie) MacSwan, worked. We three Buffington women would steam into the shop, located in a charmingly remodeled old house.

"Lois, how nice to see you! Judy, how have you been?" Jack would emerge from behind the counter to greet us. "Sally, I hope you can find some things you like!" She herself was a bluff, trim woman who wore the store's classic styles with panache.

We would chat and remark on the displays and merchandise. Then, hanger by hanger, Judy and Mom would go through the sale rack while I ranged around looking at the new fall clothes and loving the color choices. The Sail Loft sold high-quality wool kilts, sweaters, and slacks, and summer cottons, too. From those hot August days, I particularly remember squirming in and out of Shetland sweaters or wool slacks in the fitting rooms.

When I had decided on something, Mom would say, "Oh, that looks so nice on you, Sally! Would you like it for Christmas?"

The first visit or two, though surprised to be asked to wait, I said politely, "Oh, yes, Mom, thank you!" Judy answered the same way.

After a couple of years, however, I said instead, "I'd like to wear this outfit this fall, Mom. I'll just buy it myself."

Surprised at my demur, she answered, "Won't it be too warm in California then?"

"No, remember, we're in northern California and the wind sweeps in over the bay! Besides, this sweater's so pretty, I want to wear it as soon as I can."

Wait for Christmas? Mom could easily afford to just give us the clothes. But what bothered me, though I would not have articulated it then, was the control being exercised. I felt as though she had said, "You can have what you want, but I will say when you get it." Had Christmas been a month away, I would have shrugged this off, but four months? If this gift expressed loving, it came with conditions, though I doubt Mom conceived of it that way. Looking back now, perhaps I was being petty. Yet her offer gave a mixed message, a phenomenon I kept struggling with.

Mom could be so much fun, so quick on the uptake, her lively mind and memory at the ready. She loved to discuss people and family history and had a great sense of humor. I prize a snapshot someone took of her essaying a mock can-can in the living room, laughing uproariously as she balanced on umbrellas held cane-like in each hand. And then there was that rainy night when Mom and Pete and I walked back from a social event in the village and she kept giggling and dancing a two-step around the puddles.

Once I found a tattered Victorian-era songbook on the bookshelf, and Mom and I leafed through it together. Many of the songs were outdated, quaint, or hopelessly sentimental. To my surprise, when we came to *Did You Ever Think When the Hearse Goes By*, Mom launched into a multi-verse rendition, her eyes snapping with delight. At the words "The worms crawl in/the worms crawl out/the ants play pinochle/on your snout," she winked at me conspiratorially, her voice husky and whispery.

Yet you might be enjoying her, or just relaxing in general, when a verbal barb came at you from out of nowhere. For instance, one evening before dinner everyone else was having a gin and tonic and I asked for sherry. Mom muttered grimly, "You must be crazy." Or the time when we had gotten dressed up to go somewhere, she glanced over at me and said, "You're not wearing that awful blue stuff on your eyelids, are you?"

Much of the time, these comments were little things, yet they kept me feeling unsettled, especially as Andy and I kept coming to the cottage from such a great distance. Also, Mom expressed her remarks and opinions so forcefully.

When we brought our daughters to Craigville, I felt pressure to bring them up right; inevitably, I suppose, because of the sixty-year generation gap and living in California, I was thought to be too permissive. I struggled especially with Anne in her toddler years, and Mom's "Can't you stop that child from crying?" did not help.

The worst thing, though, was Mom saying, more than once, "I'm glad I had boys. I don't care for girls." Or simply, "I don't like girls." Her beloved granddaughter Joanna (Jo) also puzzled over this. At those moments, I felt helpless. *What can I possibly do about that? It's not my fault.*

On our visits, I managed to keep the peace. But usually sometime in the last couple of days, Mom and I would end up in a verbal spat of some sort, incidents that always put poor Andy smack in the middle.

Most of the time, I fell in with what was going on. Custom—or "the way we've always done it"—extended to many other family choices, too, most of all where we swam. Once I asked if we might go to Lake Wequaquet, an inviting body of water we often drove past.

Mom's reply: "Whyever would we do that? We have the beach right here."

I said, "We don't always have to go to the same place, do we? Besides, the lake looks like wonderful swimming."

"We prefer salt water." In a matter-of-fact tone.

She meant Craigville Beach. The Beach.

The Association Beach at Craigville, also known as CBA, was and is a local institution. Five minutes' walk away, our beach bathhouse (number #142, combination 33-19-9) was another Buffington address. Family friends came and sat around chatting under our umbrella. Once beyond infant and toddler stages, the kids ranged all over playing with their friends. Mom used to bring along her needlepoint, Judy, books, and Pete, magazines and papers. One snapshot captures a family friend hooking a rug. Dad stuck around, agreeable and conversational. Group pictures in bathing suits were obligatory.

People even went swimming sometimes.

In my early years there, I used to feel self-conscious sitting around in a bathing suit all day, though I did my best socializing with people who had known each other for decades. As the new daughter-in-law, I think I made the expected responses with the proper smile. The whole milieu was like that of a pool or golf course at a country club. The bright spot was that the swimming at Craigville is superb: lovely buoyant water with little tidal variation, so you can always swim. In addition, the bottom is soft and sandy and seldom is there any undertow or current.

The Association Beach today is much the same as when I first swam there decades ago. You enter a neat wooden building, now painted gray, with long wings of bath houses extending out on either side. The same families camp on the uniform sand all day, in the same spot every summer. Public beaches on either side share the water, so our lifeguards take up their megaphones to diplomatically (but firmly) send people off our floats and back to the beach they swam or walked over from.

I soon learned that much about this place stemmed from work done by my father-in-law. In both the village of Craigville and the beach, Dad found a place that he loved and thought worth preserving, and he stuck with it. Long-time chair of the governing board, Dad was the soul of Craigville. Ever so patiently, over the decades, he coped with all the personalities and local ruckuses and worked behind the scenes to get things done.

So it is appropriate that I often remember him as he swam there. I loved to watch him. From water's edge, he would walk in a few steps, to mid-thigh or waist, then bow slightly, arcing his arms over his head, and dive. Every motion followed neatly and economically on the previous one. He cleaved the water with no splash, as though it were gel rather than liquid. Once back up from under, he quickly shook his head dry, then swam forward in a crawl with strokes like luxuriant slow flourishes. (Andy remembers Dad doing the sidestroke rather than the crawl, but the character of his motion was the same either way.) In those moments, he seemed of the water. After a while, Dad would swim back in, then stand chatting in shallow water, his voice always quiet and modulated.

Unfortunately, though, right from the start, I disliked the bath houses. Yes, they were convenient, but what a blight on the land. I hope I made this comment only to Andy: "I wish someone would just put a match to them some dark night."

I had to be careful, though, because of a sign you see today as you enter the beach precincts: Buffington Pavilion. Dad richly deserved that tribute, even as he would have been embarrassed by it while alive. He wanted no reward; however, he once said if one were inevitable, he would prefer something like a plaque "on a boiler in the basement."

Of even temperament, also utter integrity, Dad was a gentleman of the old school, one of those people you trusted. Thinking of him, I found words like "probity" and "dignity" coming to mind. Handsome and courteous, he was a wonderful listener who once told Andy, "You don't have to explain anything you didn't say."

Over time, I think Dad allowed his vivacious wife and sons to do pretty much all the talking. Even as I liked and revered him, I never felt I knew him. His thoughts always lay behind those wise gray eyes, under the shelves of salt-and-pepper brows.

He was also determinedly benign. From childhood years, Andy remembers Dad's repeatedly telling his three sons, "If you can't say anything nice, don't say anything at all!" A corollary to this was my sister-in-law Judy's comment, "I wish he could just say 'Damn!' once in a while, like the rest of us!"

In living by this philosophy, Dad had a counterpart in my mother. I have said little about her thus far, for she seldom came to Craigville and lived about forty minutes' drive away in a different part of Cape Cod. Like Dad, she was one of the quiet family sustainers—and she planted in me an outlook that affected my interactions with Andy's mom as long as I went to Craigville.

I had always leaned on my mother. Like Andy's dad, she kept things going with little fanfare. Though intelligent, also thoughtful and spiritual, Mommy minimized her role and took little credit for these qualities.

After my father died in 1979, prematurely, of a brain tumor, Mommy quietly kept on with life until 1987, when to everyone's surprise including her own, she remarried. In becoming Mrs. Ronald Leutwyler, she moved across the street to live in Ron's house and they had ten good years together. Quite naturally, she gave herself to her new husband, so my relationship with her rather diminished. Also,

Ron had never had children and was thus unused to them, so our visits sometimes became extremely awkward, though we all tried hard.

During one of my Craigville stays, I had driven over to see Mommy one day, in need of consolation after a sharp disagreement with Andy's mother.

"Oh, Sally, don't antagonize Lois!"

I no longer remember anything else she said. The message? "Don't make waves." Her advice was typical and (I suppose) practical while I stayed at the cottage accepting Mom's hospitality; probably Mommy felt I was overreacting. Yet her words (and how she had acted over the years) told me that anger or hurt were out of bounds and not proper responses. *Placate, just settle . . . don't stand up for yourself . . . and certainly never attempt to work anything out.*

Advice which my in-law family seemed already to have long since adopted. As far as I could see, then or later, what Mom said, went. With few exceptions, at least while I was on hand, no one seems to have tried to change things or negotiate disagreements in the cottage. In spite of being so highly verbal, no one talked about feelings or behavior or acted as though things might be done differently—and Mom was the last person you expected to negotiate with. Once at the cottage, married or not, the "boys" were boys again and Mom ruled. I should fit in, too.

For all her autonomy and authority, though, Mom depended on Dad. But sadly, starting in about 1980, his health declined, and he died in 1982. At a loving memorial service for him that August in the Craigville Tabernacle, Andy (piano) and I performed Bach and Handel that Dad had loved, and also a piece that Andy himself had composed.

The summers that followed were hard on Mom, who kept the cottage going pretty much on her own. Pete came from New York nearly every weekend, Andy and I continued our annual visits, and Jim and Judy did their best to lend support, though they had moved to a year-round home about forty-five minutes' drive away, in another part of Cape Cod. Thus, when I visited Craigville, Mom and I were cast in together. She became, in effect, my dominant parent.

Even twenty years after my father's death, I still missed him. He was the one I had always looked for first thing when we flew back. The moment I landed at Logan Airport, once I had made my way out to the waiting area, I would search for him and lock in with his eyes.

Back in the days when there were observation decks in airports, I once spotted him even before we landed. As our plane descended, Daddy stood out there in the wind. Knobby knees exposed by khaki shorts, his arms folded, his eyes searched the skies. Though he couldn't know which plane I was on or which miniscule window I was peering through, he was looking for me. And there he was: the person who always loved me. I had him! The only person who called me "Sal."

I will never land in Boston without missing him.

Missing the first person in my life whose mind I ever truly communicated with. My father was a mix of parent, hero, teacher, co-conspirator, book lover, classical music afficionado, correspondent—and Cape Codder. Though neither of us were natives, Daddy and I took to the Cape as soon as we moved there and started exploring together.

Whenever I returned, we kept on doing as much as we could of these things, even if equal family time allowed us only a couple of hours some afternoons. The best thing was a late-night discussion across the living room. His wide forehead gleaming in the lamplight, my father would stretch out in his big old chair, with his old yellow cat poured over one knee, all four paws and tail hanging down. As we talked, Daddy would gently whomp Toby on the rump—"Nice pusser!"—and the cat purred away.

Always my father had a book "to chew over" with me, or a question about what I was doing or my teaching; or he wanted to talk about his beloved California, both the old days and how I was finding it now. Or he wanted to take me to some new Cape Cod place or trail or landing or explain or discuss some intriguing local phenomenon.

Daddy was Cape Cod.

But now my primary parent was a mercurial and confounding person. At times I felt that Mom was still bringing me up. Expressing love or reinforcement was not her style, yet she needed support, too. And at the same time she was aging, so was the house we shared.

Yet I was coming to love this roomy barn of a place. Beautiful any time of day, as you woke in the morning with sunlight shining in, or as you returned from an evening walk, coming up the path to where lamps glowed like lanterns inside.

Craigville: a house full of travel souvenirs from the days before Pier One and World Market, bought in foreign places and shipped home like trophies of the hunt bagged by Mom. A house so full of dishes and glassware that major dinner parties were possible every night. Cape Cod air filled the house, too, as did old games and a crazy collection of straw hats for the beach. A house full of chat over drinks on the porch or conversation in the kitchen while cooking got done or over washing up the dishes. A house with scads of old chairs, tables piled with *New Yorkers* and *National Geographics*, and shelves groaning under the old 78 record albums. A house surrounded by porches, lawn, and clotheslines full of socks, sheets, and towels, its bedrooms full of people, bedrooms from whose ceilings hung old wooden model airplanes. A house whose stash of old toys included both manufactured blocks and leftover wood scraps from various projects, also a heroic old metal fire engine. A house on Cape Cod in which you could find album after album of old snapshots and see the men and women from past decades in long white skirts and dresses or absurd bathing costumes—all posing on the front porch or lawn, having fun just as this family was now. Craigville! A house of people at play, enjoying the good old summertime, just as it had always been and always would be. Craigville.

BLUEBERRY PIE

One of the great old dishes, blueberry pie is almost "as American as apple pie." A good one is simply wonderful.

And Mom's blueberry pie was terrific.

So much so that in about ten minutes, all her hours of work came down to a mess of scraped plates. We should have been required to take a single mouthful per minute—no, every five minutes—to fully appreciate and savor those pies. But even that would not have been long enough.

Rich, dark, and lively, almost like a preserve, a forkful was not so much a mix of tastes as a concentrated sensation. We all consumed each slice as though in a collective bite and then were rewarded with a glorious aftertaste.

Those pies were made of blueberries from the dozen or so bushes on the wooded slopes down toward the marsh. Though the woods were lovely, berry picking was a chore; the weather was often hot and humid, and black flies, horse flies, and mosquitos kept you company. As for finding the fruit, the berries were seldom where your eyes or hands thought they were. You had to constantly change focal length to locate them. In addition, each berry had to be pried from its socket and each came from studded twigs in starbursts; each twiglet bore three or four tiny berries. You did not automatically pick a whole twiglet, either, for the berries on each one ranged from cool green to semi-ripe plum to deep indigo blue. A lot of selectivity was required.

Swooping in from the sky, the birds left peck marks on rejected berries; they, too, found unripe berries tart. As for human pickers, most of us helped out at one time or another, but Mom and Pete were the real hunter-gatherers. Distracted by the beauty of the sun-dappled woods, I loved the crumply sound of walking on dry leaves and the papery fragrance my footsteps released, and I just could not summon up enough patience. And supposedly, I was on vacation; I wanted to enjoy myself.

Not so Pete and Mom! Clad in ratty old clothes (including a paint-spattered old tuxedo shirt), Pete's hands swarmed the branches as he filled a measuring cup. Occasionally, though, he would slow down and get lost in thought; sometimes he stopped entirely. For Mom, blueberries meant stages: picking, sorting, pie assembly, and freezing berries for Thanksgiving or Christmas feasts.

Mom recorded each summer's total harvest in a little notebook, cup by cup, even by quarter cups some summers. After a big berry year, the next summer might yield few berries or none at all. Apparently ground and bushes would be exhausted; she described one summer as "A virtual wipeout."

1976 was the record year: "26 quarts total."

1988 came pretty close, though: "23 qts., 3/4 cup."

1991: "Bushes near house are loaded with berries . . . getting more sun with so much leaf canopy lost to Hurricane Bob."

1992: "Very cool summer; slow to ripen, the first quantities we pick can be measured in numbers of berries."

I wish I could have conferred on her Thoreau's luck: "Sometimes copious rains early in August will cause those masses of small green berries . . . to swell and ripen every one so that their harvest fulfills the promise of their spring."

A single Craigville pie was made up of fruit so small that its contents could be measured in the thousands of berries: dark blue things about the size of a peppercorn, which someone's thumb and finger had gently pinched then dropped in an old tin cup hooked over a belt so as to leave hands free. Next, dumped into a colander, they were rinsed and dried inside a crumpled-up dishtowel. Then they landed on old dark brown cookie sheets that Mom used for sorting. Late in the afternoon you would find her on the porch, gin and tonic at hand, her fingertips hovering an inch above the spread of rolling berries to cull any duds. So, depending on the generosity of harvest, the berry content of the pie might translate into anywhere from one to four hours of labor.

For the pie crust, Mom relied on a Fanny Farmer recipe, I think from the 1926 edition of *The Boston Cooking-School Cookbook*. Working at the white enamel-top kitchen table, she rolled out on the surface, having made pastry earlier and chilled it for easy handling. A pie required simple ingredients: flour, salt, shortening (Crisco), and a little water for the crust; then the blueberries, sugar, and some sort of thickening. The magic was in her skill, and in the pungent wild fruit whose spicy fragrance perfumed the kitchen during baking.

At dinner that evening, the main course done and cleared, Mom would place the rumply crusted pie on the table, then sit down to a chorus of comments that amounted to purrs. "I've been looking forward to this all day!" from Pete at the far end and "Gee, Grammy, that looks wonderful!" from Katherine.

First counting heads, Mom then fractioned the pie into slices, including one or two pieces for seconds. No one ever asked for a sliver. As the plates were passed, slices received and forked into, conversation pretty much stopped. Until the next chorus.

"Wow! Mom, this is simply wonderful!"

"You make the best, Grammy!"

"Well, the crust isn't quite up to my usual standard but . . ."

"It's as perfect as ever. Don't change a thing!"

Clinking and scraping across china.

Then Mom asked, "Who'd like another piece? Or shall I split one of these?"

Who most deserved a second piece, who had worked hardest that day? Someone who had mowed the lawn in hot sun or someone just arrived after a long drive or bus trip? Whatever the decision, no pie was ever left over . . . though maybe a skim of juice and an orphan berry or two still clung to the pie plate.

One evening Joanna (then in her twenties) leaned over, grabbed the plate, and started scraping with a spoon. Soon, though, she said, "That doesn't work" and, to a burst of laughter, picked up the plate in both hands and licked out every last smidge. Someone taunted, "Piggy!"

Mom beamed, saying, "Don't miss that bit over there!" and pointed to a remaining spot of juice. Another night, another summer, Katherine happily licked the plate.

As for commercial berries, Mom did not approve. "Oh, those haven't any flavor, they're just mush!" Occasionally she used wild ones for color in fruit compotes, but their sourness stood out because sugar did not penetrate the skins unless the berries were cooked.

Not only did I find the sweetness of store-bought berries tempting, but they also represented ease and convenience. Though some pie-labor got integrated into daily life or Mom did other tasks during certain stages, such as chilling the crust or oven baking, those pies made for an awful lot of work.

I am not sure whether Mom liked picking berries, either, but she dragooned us all into it and upbraided us when we were less than eager. I think her attitude was a throwback: use what is provided, what the land supplies. Also, do not waste anything. And when I helped with shopping and tried to suggest buying commercial berries, I knew that she controlled the purse strings as well as the choices—and I, too, loved the pies.

They spoke of an earlier time when everyone worked and worked with little thought of how demanding or time-consuming household jobs were, when the family did all its own repairs and painting (though perhaps not steep roofs or entire houses), and no one balked at caulking or carrying out meticulous closing procedures. In those early cottage years, if you had the materials or ingredients on hand, you just plunged in and made or did something, no matter what. Everyone's time was cheap. Mom often reminded us how easy we had it, compared to her and Dad's early married years during the Depression.

Yet the time for such economy was long past, and the family had grown prosperous. I often felt that such work was a show of loyalty or done to prove you loved the cottage. Mom and I were living through a generational change, with blueberry pies as one of the happier, certainly the more delicious, manifestations of the old way. I think of the words of the old hymn, "Awake, awake to love and work . . . spend thyself nor count the cost."

But I did count the cost. I could not manage this throwing all one's resources into household tasks. And here I was alongside this person, my mother-in-law, much older than me, who was working like a Trojan. How could I let the side down by not pitching in, or even want to spend time contemplatively?

Work was both the method and the major ingredient of blueberry pie.

WRITING

All my Craigville summer experiences, however, rested on two foundations: distance and letters home. From California, I sent weekly accounts of our lives; Mom and my mother wrote back, and my father did, too. We supplemented these writings with long distance calls, always chatting with a weather eye on the clock.

Mom's letters, though, achieved a higher level than the usual family letters: the family regarded her as having credentials. After majoring in Journalism at Northwestern, she had worked three years at the *Minneapolis Star* as society editor before marrying Dad, but she never worked professionally after that.

Perhaps it is not surprising then that Mom's letters looked like newspapers. Whether typed on her beloved Olympia portable or handwritten, they consumed entire pages; no need for margins. Her style was detailed, well-organized, and crisp, as though her letters were expert productions and the rest of us were her readership.

Long before I met her, Mom, too, had written home. Letter writing was simply part of daily life. All through my growing up years, I had watched my mother and grandmother keep up fervent correspondence with their English relatives. When Grammie quoted or read aloud entire blue airmail letters from her half-sister and old friends, their words seemed alive; it was as though she were participating in a sudden séance. She wrote back in the same frame of mind. After all, her hand, any writer's hand, touched and inscribed the paper that was to fly to the hand of the person receiving it.

Yet that metaphorical arm's length stretched out many thousands of miles, and even though letters were common then, not every piece of correspondence held sway. Sometimes I quickly scanned letters and didn't stop to analyze the personality behind them. Especially in my heady early years in California, I think I missed clues to relationship, such as Mom's caustic though witty comments, because they were not directed at me nor delivered with her trademark spoken vehemence.

In person, at Craigville, however, she and I had to make it up as we went along. There I had no choice but to notice and feel her tone, and of course I might disagree with her.

Ultimately all our letters represented the continent's worth of distance between us. Yet my father had said a few days before Andy and my wedding, "We'll miss you like hell, Sal, but you're doing the right thing to get away."

Mom also did much writing of another kind in The Red Notebook: the Bible, if you will, of Craigville. Still in Andy and my possession, the Red Notebook is a spiral-bound affair in which Mom and Dad and other family members recorded how they bought and kept the house, line by line, cost by cost, word by word. A local reference, the Red Notebook was repeatedly hauled out for accurate information and correcting memory.

Genesis 1:1. "1938: Purchased cottage from Aunt Annie for $2500."

Next entry, same page. "Mom Buff gave us iron twin beds . . . bought inner spring mattresses, $56.00. Arthur Cobb reroofed the cottage . . . plus replacing back steps. $200."

Bed, board, and roof—how much more basic can you get? The necessary elements for summer to have its special, dedicated home. From there on out, the notebook got loaded with canceled checks, taped-in business cards, receipts, and bills ranging from sixty-nine cents to several thousand dollars. Also detailed accounts of jobs, long before the term "sweat equity" was coined. Some years, the pages were crammed, though during the WWII years of gas rationing and mostly women and children on hand, apparently there wasn't time to do much to the house, let alone record anything. Later, the occasional family milestone got noted, too, such as "Peter made Vice Pres." My daughter Katherine's birth got noted on the 1976 page, between lawn mower repair at Sears and the purchase of pyracantha bushes.

As far as detail is concerned, Mom's entries take the prize, and sometimes they possess a charm all of their own. Referring to window painting and caulking (an endless parade of fussy jobs until modern windows were installed), Mom noted ". . . paint was all curled up and peeling. If this was part of 1977 paint job, it was a miserable failure."

Mom also noted, "Raccoon came down chimney in dining room and clawed Victorian sofa and large chair. Mended chair with Press-on tape but had to have sofa reupholstered. 4 yds. yellow damask nylon $24.00."

Reporting on raking lawn clippings with Pete, she recorded that they "created Monet-like haystacks." Her entries often consume many lines, her flourishy handwriting matches her descriptive flair.

I must, however, give Dad a nod for one of my favorite entries: "Dining room clock laid down and died."

Most of all, though, Mom poured herself into her letters; also, she saved some, including an account of Andy's birth, which she later gave to me. In her final years, those letters were gallant indeed and often full of irreverent humor. Of a blood clot, Mom wrote, "The x-rays of course reminded me of an airview of the Mississippi river system with all its tributaries." Or on having a bug, "People love to tell you, 'Oh, there's a lot of that going around,' as if it was a supernatural gremlin just pouncing to make people's lives uncomfortable."

At times she took a self-deprecating tone: "This letter reminds me of _____'s speeches. He was really a darling, full of good humor, jokes and warm heartedness, but if you were trying to write a newspaper account, you simply could not pin down a thing he had said. Thus what news I have is really just fluff . . . ." Not true. Alert and observant, Mom was far too definite, well-organized, and intelligent for that.

Reading her travel reports, you took the trip with her. Anything but "Oh, it was marvelous," you knew who took the cruise with her, whose table to avoid at dinner. She reported details that made you wonder if she had interviewed the people in question. Postcards, she filled to the max—she once crammed in twenty-seven lines on one. And the blue airmail folders she wrote on must have sighed with relief when she scribbled "Love from Mom and Dad" down at the bottom, her cramped letters barely squeezing in along the final crease of thin paper.

In 1992, I joined this travel account tradition when I shared my twenty-five-page journal of a trip to England, a landmark journey set in motion by my mother to help Andy and me and our kids renew our ties to my English heritage and Braithwaite family. An ambitious trip nearly a month long, it stretched us all. For me, it was a Grand Tour of a kind.

After reading my account, Mom commented that I had written "so that many years from now she [Sally] can recapture exactly how she felt at a given place." Which was, to a great degree, just what I wanted to do. The trip left me with marvelous memories, of course, but also a record beyond letters, a valued personal narrative.

With this account, was I unconsciously competing with Mom? Or acting on the human tendency to hold onto experience by writing and go beyond just "Oh, I remember . . ."? Some of both, I think.

This travel journal of mine was significant, too, in that it commemorated almost the only summer of our marriage that I did not go to Craigville. (Of necessity, we had also skipped 1976, too, when Katherine was born that July.) And though I did not know it at the time, my 1992 account presaged yet another birth: an essay I would write the following year, about Craigville itself—and the major change of focus going on in my life.

During the 1990s, I was not only experiencing the menopause but also starting to carry out a big change in my professional life. I had come to want a divorce. Not from Andy, but from the flute, which by then I had taught and performed on for thirty-some years. The instrument seemed no longer to express who I was; its intrinsic sound seemed sweet, jejune— after all, I had chosen it back in fourth grade. Now I was meeting up with a new stage of life, demanding and often dark, as the nineties featured many deaths of family and friends to whom I was close.

I had also come to want to create what I worked on, rather than presenting someone else's creative product—and I dreamed of making something which would last. Pleasing though I might sound on the flute, all my notes floated off into the air and disappeared.

So, having long been a fanatic reader and also a keeper of journals, and with word processing newly and readily available (a huge liberation), I began to write essays and poems. I attended several workshops and joined a writing group. I was reading many books of women's letters and diaries, also finding myself in the explosion of personal memoirs then coming out. The writings of Anne Morrow Lindbergh particularly inspired me, with their focus on domestic life.

In other words, feelings: that private-become-public area which I think worried not just Mom but the whole Buffington family. The emotional stuff that you did not speak about, the difficult things that were better left buried. The subjects you could not get hold of or trust, unlike home repairs or history or travel.

Mom probably felt she had been doing this kind of writing for years, in those letters. Perhaps her thoughts ran along the lines of, *Domestic stuff is just for family. Nobody else needs to know. Why is Sally thinking she should write about her life and her doings? Why should anyone else care?*

To her, I think writing had become simply a tool, a well-learned one at that, and "nothing to write home about." Yet it was a passion I was growing into.

I no longer remember when or what I told Mom about changing careers, but I do remember the message I received. "Stick to what you were trained for, you don't get to change." Perhaps she had been disappointed at someone else's having abandoned an expensive college education or training, but she loudly disapproved of anyone doing other than what he or she had started out to do. I wonder now if her private reaction was something like, *Oh, no. Writing—that will just divert Sally from what she's already doing and her family responsibilities. Besides, it'll send her mind off on anything but what we need around here. What a foolish idea!*

In contemplating such a change, I was inspired by my father, who had also made a major change in mid-life. In addition, I still missed his encouraging, loving attitude. "You can do it, Sal. I'll follow and watch and be interested, no matter what you do."

Yet to be fair, way back, Mom herself had probably had any sense of possibility, career-wise, closed to her. She professed not to mind that she never worked again after marrying Dad, but I have often wondered how true that was.

She did appreciate fine creative work; for instance, one year I was so impressed by Ivan Doig's *This House of Sky* that I gave it to her for Christmas. Mom thanked me so fervently I thought, *Good! That really worked!*

But more than once, she also conveyed the idea that for me, or for her, or for anyone other than some professors of her acquaintance, to write books or essays or poems and put them out there, was crazy. My feelings or ideas would never reach those high standards, I was not famous and could not become so, and therefore I shouldn't even try.

Or was the problem distrust of feelings and her own inner thoughts? Her reading offers some clues. Mom loved nonfiction by John McPhee, also biography and history in general; she avoided and disavowed fiction and poetry, though in her last years, she did enjoy Jane Austen.

One summer, I attended the Creative Nonfiction Writing workshop at Goucher College; McPhee was the keynote speaker. While I studied under a different writer there, of course I attended his reading and afterward stood in line to get a book autographed for Mom. On arriving at Craigville later that summer, I gave it to her. Quickly, she unwrapped the book then tucked it away without comment.

As surprised as I was, Pete spoke up. "Ma, Sally's brought you a book by John McPhee—and it's autographed, too!"

She muttered a brief thanks, then, "I've already read that one!"

I have wondered ever since if Mom was envious that I and not she had met this man she revered. Or if, deep inside, she wished she could write books like that, expressive of her rangy mind and intelligence.

When I spoke passionately about memoir and poetry, I think I ran counter to her "Just the facts, Ma'am" training and way of thinking; both, especially poetry, deal with imagination, feelings, even an artsy world view. As Patricia Hampl has put it, ". . . to make a metaphor is to make a fuss . . . poetry, with its tendency to make connections and to break the barriers between past and present [is] slightly embarrassing."

Yet intuitively connecting or juxtaposing things fascinated me; such writing was what I responded to most and was setting out to do.

ALL THE YEARS
OF SUMMER

*I*n June 1993, I wrote an essay titled *All the Years of Summer* and gave it to Mom for her birthday in June, to celebrate and thank her. Twenty-two hundred words of my impressions of Craigville, I had worked on the piece all that spring. Though I felt some trepidation about making such an offering, Andy encouraged me to go ahead and also urged me to share it with the rest of the family.

Here are some quotes.

"I first saw our cottage at Craigville on a raw gray day in the winter of 1968, when Andy and I were newly engaged. The house stood bleakly on the hill among bare trees . . . ."

A few paragraphs later. "I can right this minute draw a map of the whole property . . . . I can precisely locate the blueberry bushes, or private landmarks such as the place where I once saw a cardinal, or the elegant red fox one summer. I can feel the grass or pine needles or the pebbly old concrete walks on the soles of my feet . . . .

"If you walk in the plopping rain, sloshing about as my daughter Anne does, there is a shiny glaze on the leaves . . . they're like freshly washed spinach. After the rain, the freshness is so total and palpable, you feel you are striding through drifts of invisible mist."

However, my writing betrayed little if any hesitation or worry. I even gave the house itself a voice.

". . . if the house could speak, it might say, 'Well, here I am. I may not be fancy, but I am rich in the times of this family and its friends. I am as seasoned as the old tongue-in-groove wood in my upstairs rooms. Every year, another layer of events settles on me, and in my dowager fashion, I become even more valued and cherished . . . ."

Another page, back to my own thoughts. "I know the familiar arrangement of furniture and the cast of characters that walk that stage! I am one of them and Andy and I have added two more, our daughters Katherine and Anne. I know the bursting vitality of the place, all the fun we have there. So often I think back to it, to the stored-up richness . . . ."

Richness? Oh, yes! By now, I had been visiting and observing for twenty-five years. But how about my authoritative tone? Whose house was this?

"The furnishings are a comfortable mixture a decorator would call eclectic. I can see them all as I write . . . . There's a big kitchen with two pantries, leading to the dining room, which has been known to seat twelve or fourteen. The favored place, though, is The Porch— the screened section that faces west. We all gravitate there, to write postcards, talk, shell peas, do needlework, read the mail, or just sit and listen to the trees.

"Surrounding our cottage is Cape Cod's beauty . . . green marsh reeds and grass, dark mud, and the river; salty fresh air . . . on bright summer and fall days everything is blown clean, sky and ocean paintbox blue; every detail stands out so sharply, that for a moment life itself seems simple and clear.

"I also revisit occasions and moments, and recall so many people, our times together. . . .

Many times around the big table come to mind . . . messy lobster feasts, vociferous dinners. I remember Amy and Lisa, Katie and Ben, Katherine and Anne all scoffing down pizza while telling jokes and family secrets at a birthday party . . . . I can taste other good things, too—swordfish, gin and tonics, corn on the cob, beach plum jelly, ice cream from the Four Seas . . . summer food . . . . I remember cooking with Judy and Mom one afternoon, joking that we felt like farm wives preparing for husbands to return from harvesting. The menfolk were occupied taking down a tree or some such job that day."

In all, I took quite the overview. "No, we do not always get along perfectly. This is not a Norman Rockwell family. We are all strong individuals who sometimes disagree. Good will gets strained by differing lifestyles thrown together. Babies do cry and children get bored and fussy on long rainy days. Surely, I am not the only one who has taken long stalking walks on the beach road, to calm and defuse anger. But we come back and try again. There is a sense of long continuity to the place—which both reassures and presses in at times."

The essay had been written as a gift, in gratitude. But I got to the thanking part only on page four, after roaring along with my own thoughts for quite a while.

"The great sustainer is Mom. She keeps it all going in a practical way and did so long before I started coming. Keeping a big house and family organized, attending to all the details that make it possible for us to enjoy ourselves—she has given us this immense gift of self and dedication for over 50 years . . . I have written this piece to thank her, but it is not enough . . . A real return would be for someone in the family to do what she has done, to take over the running of Craigville when she no longer can or wishes to and continue its role as Buffington family center.

". . . this summer place is a resource for us all. It gives a blessing, a grace to our everyday lives, because it is waiting there and we can harken back to it whenever we wish. I cherish many pictures of Craigville, but my favorite one is this: the porch in the late afternoon, our lively figures silhouetted against the changing sky charged with light. The trees rustle with the breeze and birds call around us. We are all laughing and talking over the day, drinks in hand, enjoying each other.

"We will keep going there, recreating this picture and making new ones. Every summer will take the sheets off the furniture, make its rooms livable again. Every summer we can renew ourselves in this haven that Mom and Dad began, thankful for the blending of fun, natural beauty, and our family together that is Craigville."

The day after her birthday, Mom wrote me, "I was immensely touched at your unusual birthday present and its laudatory view of me as Queen Mother at the Craigville cottage . . . . I have always regarded myself as the top sergeant in its everyday operations."

She went on to cite Judy's and my "easy going . . . skills to make entertaining the relaxed fun it should be." Then, as usual, she reported on her doings: having friends over, her other grandchildren, events at her retirement complex, and plans for the coming summer at Craigville. She closed, "Again, thank you for your special efforts to make my birthday memorable. Love, Mom."

A few days later, sister-in-law Judy wrote me, "Mom was so very pleased, Sally; she professes not to be a sentimental person, but her appreciation of your work was obvious." Judy herself also thanked me profusely, as did her daughter and younger son, who wrote generous letters of thanks.

I had indeed crafted the essay carefully—but it was my take on Craigville. In places, I sound downright possessive. "I know the familiar arrangement of furniture and the cast of characters that walk that stage . . . I know the bursting vitality of the place, all the fun we have there. So often I think back to it, to the stored-up richness, which my memory eagerly supplies."

Not only was this the first time I had written my visions of Craigville, but also until then I had not realized how it was claiming me. And in spite of all these words, I did not recognize how much I had said nor how boldly I had spoken.

ESSAYING

*M*y essay was not the only event in a milestone year: on June 29, 1993, Andy and I celebrated our twenty-fifth wedding anniversary. At home in California, we delightedly threw ourselves quite the party. At Craigville, probably someone raised a toast to us; we received a couple of cards from the family and the usual "Take yourselves out to dinner" check from Mom.

We were of course expected at Craigville, and that August we spent what Andy and I thought was a happy visit—and as had become usual, the best mix we could manage of helping around the property and having some fun.

However, on August 28, Mom's and my typical almost-at-the-end clash was the worst ever. The day before Andy and I and the girls were to fly back, she let fly at me.

I have no memory of what set her off, though I do remember that she and I were standing in the dining room near the window. Mom faced me down, her dark eyes full of force, as was her voice. She stabbed out words. "Nobody wants to work around here! There's so much to do, the bathrooms need cleaning with so many people around, and there's all those loads of laundry to hang out! And look, this room needs painting! And there's those garage windows needing to be caulked." Gesturing toward the garage, out the nearby window, she took a step closer to me.

What could I say? I could not think of any nastier job than caulking the old windows. She stormed on. "But you all just want to read—or go somewhere and do tourist things. This place needs work and people who will do that. Not people who just sit around on a beautiful beach day or balk at anything more than a simple chore!"

Mom paused, perhaps for breath. "When I took Anne out to pick blueberries, she wasn't much use at all. She wouldn't keep at it, just kept drifting off into the woods. . . . And Katherine—mooning around like that, doing nothing . . . and they leave their shoes in the living room! Teenagers! And you just let them get away with it! It's that permissive California style of yours."

I looked down, aside, anywhere else than at her. I took a step back. She went on and on, her voice abrading and bitter. All I could think was, *How can I get out of here?* I felt nailed down. Her every sentence was like a wave crashing over me, holding me in her storm-field of energy. *Isn't there some way I can escape?*

Nothing I could say would do any good. I would only prolong the tirade—and much she said was not true. Over the past couple of weeks, Andy, Katherine, Anne, and I had spent hours with Mom, scraping paint, picking blueberries, cooking, making repairs, hanging out laundry, and cleaning. Working. And now such anger was coming at me, completely minus affection or understanding. Was this how Mom really felt?

"You're all wrapped up in your own lives! Well, go back to them! And get out of here and out of my house!" With this, she stalked off into the kitchen, the swinging door swishing back and forth behind her.

For the rest of the day, I stayed as far away from Mom as possible. Andy would have to interact with her. I was done. I helped the kids pack up, then got my own and Andy's things together, making super-extra-sure I was leaving nothing behind or unfinished.

That evening, I managed to record, "I got absolutely slammed by Mom's anger, the verbal gun's many barrels leveled at me at close range. Only some of the stuff was my fault at all . . . . I have never been so chewed out, so savaged, by another adult in my whole life."

By this time Mom was in her late eighties and living the rest of the year in a senior apartment complex off-Cape. Elderly though she was to manage a big cottage like Craigville, giving it up seemed out of the question, at least far as I could see. That day, I think she was tired out and couldn't manage any longer without venting.

As for my essay and the appreciation I had expressed, it seemed to have amounted to "just words." Later, puzzling over what had happened, I wondered if I had unconsciously provoked Mom's outburst. Perhaps she had read my essay as a threat and a sign that the next generation was all too ready to step up and replace her—or worse still, just keep coasting along on her management while complaining or disagreeing.

However, what I had written in *All the Years of Summer* about the cottage and its succession amounted to a kind of growing up on my part, for which perhaps no one was ready. Least of all, Mom herself. Without perceiving it, in my essay I had declared, for myself, a personal coming of age at Craigville.

From my journal, back home in California. August 31st. "I am so glad to be back in my own house . . . so much bitterness at Craigville . . . . I was trying to simply make it through in a civilized fashion . . . . I feel some pride that I did not lose my temper . . . ."

September 7. "I am still working through the trip . . . . The smallest thing, or mention of something, gets my mind wound up again . . . . I've been feeling so stung . . . just plain battered. Now I am back here and can put myself back together, I almost don't know what to do."

My first Sunday back at church, friends hugged me, saying, "Oh, Sally, it's so good to see you!" "We missed you!" Far from sounding automatic or clichéd, their words made me feel I was a good person after all and worthy of being liked. Of being included in.

Still, I felt I must write the usual thank-you letter; what came out was the shortest, most mechanical such note I had ever written.

Dear Mom,
Thank you for having us. We loved your blueberry pie. I hope
you're enjoying the quiet time. I am sorry if we made trouble for
you. Thanks for everything.
—Sally

A couple of weeks later, Mom wrote us in her usual style, a long
newsy letter, as detailed as ever, with no reference to the blowup. She
did not apologize. Did she remember the incident at all?

Though at least I had apologized, barely, I was still fighting her
inwardly. Also, I hadn't known exactly what to apologize for. I could
not change Mom, much less pretend the event had never happened,
but every day hurt and anger flooded my thinking. My mother-in-law
had taken on power over me.

After about a month, I wrote a poem in which I personified my
anger as a feral cat that had leapt onto my shoulders, then dug in with
its claws. The cat? Mom, of course, she who disliked cats all her life.

Anger Cat

I am angry at my anger

I need to shake off
This vicious feral cat
That has latched on to me.

It seems to tire slowly
Its hold weakened by time's pull

Yet still it stings me,
Still blood-bitterness
Seeps out, staining

And tainting my thoughts
Taking energy away
When I need most to love.

More than shedding
The biting clawing beast
I will throw it off!

De-claw, de-fang,
Reduce the cat
To impotent furry pet

So that I am once more
My clear unburdened self
Freed to work, to fully love.

As I worked over the poem, I calmed myself. Writing helped me to suck out the anger, though I kept most of this to myself. I wrote other poems, too, including *Disquiet*, about the atmosphere I had sensed in the cottage. Others were not getting along so well there, either, as one stanza shows.

People scrape
Against each other,
Voices competing
In a raucous choir.
My hapless notes
Make further dissonance
And are undesired.

Rereading my essay now, I think I was carried by a wave of affection for the cottage itself, a wave that might be said to have crashed. Or perhaps I caused a silent earthquake: I made a claim on Craigville whose substance seems to have gone unnoticed by everyone.

For me, the English trip the previous summer had functioned as a "Now you've seen the world" experience. I had spent a summer away from Craigville expectations, away from Mom—able to act in my usual capacity as a responsible adult.

In the essay, I took an overview and stated it confidently, writing page after page from my perspective as though I had stepped up on stage and delivered an original monologue or speech—and without

Mom's long tenure. I sounded as though I were the one who had created the cottage and its world.

My essay exemplified Joan Didion's words: "In many ways, writing is the act of saying I, of imposing oneself upon other people, of saying listen to me, see it my way, change your mind . . . there's no getting around the fact that setting words on paper is the imposition of the writer's sensibility on the reader's most private space."

Ultimately, I was coming up for air. That is, after twenty-five years of marriage and in-law membership in the Buffington family, I had begun to think, unconsciously, *Well, I have some worthy thoughts, too. I have come to love this place and have some ideas. I can speak up. I can penetrate through all the verbal display and brilliance around here because I am as smart as they are. And as important.*

FIVE MORE YEARS

I returned to Craigville the next summer (1994), though with great apprehension. However, I had been invited to play in a chamber music recital in the village and was hardly about to turn down such an opportunity, even as my interest in the flute was waning. Fortunately, the concert came off beautifully and I managed fairly well with Mom except for a minor tiff over rehearsing with the violinist in the cottage kitchen.

The following summer I brought Anne along with a friend of hers, an arrangement I had been reluctant to try before. I hoped Anne would be happier and less at loose ends this way, but the experiment was not a success. We all—Anne, Mom, and I—ended up just getting through as best we could.

From then on, only Andy and I visited; one of those years I found myself staying at the cottage with only Mom and Pete. Things thinned down, you might say, and the rest of us agreed we must make things as easy for her as possible.

Often now, I found Mom starved for conversation. Not only had she far less physical endurance, but usually she was alone in the cottage all week until Pete arrived from New York Friday nights for weekends. She would sometimes keep me at the breakfast table talking until ten or ten thirty, she who in the past would have leapt to the day's tasks as soon as possible, often as others were still finishing their coffee.

She told me stories I had never known before, some all-too-familiar ones, loads of family history, information about her friends, and her feelings about death and her time in life. Mom was holding onto every second of every day. This thorough living was admirable, also heavy on trivia. Often her talk was a version of the old phrase about impending death, "All my life flashes before me." She and I shared some happy times, with only minor disagreements. The 1993 blowup never got mentioned; I fell silent if we veered onto dangerous ground.

Also, more than once, Mom would say something like, "All I did today was walk to the post office, then be driven around with you, walk and shop a little—and I'm exhausted."

Evenings, Andy and I might take an after-dinner walk. Coming back up the path, we would find Mom in her living room chair, in a little circle of light amid the dark house. Her feet rested on the needlepoint-covered footstool, her shoes set neatly off to the side. Deep in the latest *New Yorker*, her brows knitted and formed an almost straight line across her face; a translucent fluff of white hair surrounded her head. In the harsh light, her facial features appeared strong, her bones more prominent, with nothing soft but her cloud of white hair.

As soon as the screen door slammed behind us, it was clear Mom was itching to talk. As I listened, I began to think that the life force in her was concentrated in rushes of words. Her sentences piled on top of each other as though her life were a reel unwinding. Nothing she said was halfway; every thought and opinion was strongly voiced.

Though Mom began to find cooking tiring, she kept at it. I helped whenever I could. By this time, though, Mom often asked me to cook dinner and entertain friends for her—but I did not take on making pies. She still wanted to do those herself.

As Mom worked at the kitchen table, I heard her mutter, "I just can't see in here, the light's terrible!" The kitchen seemed bright enough to me, but her eyesight must have been worse than I knew. Perhaps the color of the pastry blended all too well with the white enamel tabletop. Or was the perpetual tremor in her hands more troublesome than ever? At any rate, making pie took her twice as long it used to; the whole process was heroic. But she was determined.

As we ate the pie, she said, "Too much sugar!"

"No, Mom, it's as good as ever! Absolutely delicious!"

"It's wonderful!"

She shook her head. Later I heard her mutter, "I've lost my touch with pastry."

Still, she picked blueberries and noticed the lack of enthusiasm in the rest of us. Frequently she warned, "I know, I can tell, when I'm gone, none of you will pick blueberries anymore! They'll just wither on the bushes."

In those final years, Mom experienced several of the mini-strokes known as TIAs. One night I was staying with my mother in Brewster when Pete called about ten P.M. to say that Mom had been taken to Cape Cod Hospital in an ambulance. I rushed over, keeping iron control on myself not to speed or make a wrong turn. Reaching her bedside, I found Mom recovered, sitting up and chatting away, delighted to see me. She wrote me later, "If there ever is another such episode, I do hope someone will remember to bring along a magazine or book for me to read in the all-alone waits before the various staff people come in to do their things and vanish. They all hustled in and out . . . somehow it reminded me of *Alice in Wonderland*."

In 1998, which turned out to be her last summer at Craigville, I heard Mom tell a friend as I drove them both to lunch, "Sometimes I feel I'm doing so little, there's no use in my keeping on living. I get very depressed sometimes."

Her friend Florence agreed.

Mom went on, "But if there were a door marked EXIT and I could take it, I don't know if I would."

She continued to write us long, fascinating letters. Reporting on her dentist rebuilding two of her teeth: "Seemed like he was dismantling the Berlin Wall . . . I've got to live five more years just to get the value out of his work." Referring to some stitches to be removed after an eye operation, she wrote, "In some lights they look like glittering sequins, and then there is a space which looks as if embroidery had been done."

Whatever her physical problems, her whimsy was undiminished. One year, along with Christmas money gifts, she sent a check to our dog. "Pay to the order of: CHESTER BUFFINGTON, 2,000 bones."

In spite of vision and hearing difficulties, Mom kept going places, including a van excursion to the Museum of Fine Arts in Boston late in 1998, about six months before she died. "I cannot ever recall so completely relishing an exhibit of paintings as these wonderfully serene and luminous Fitz Hugh Lane pictures. . . spent 1¾ hours just drinking it in." I wish I had been with her.

By this time in her life, Mom often had to say final goodbyes to friends and acquaintances. Writing us of one funeral, she mentioned the hymns *Amazing Grace*, predictably enough, and *Softly and Tenderly Jesus Is Calling*. She wrote, "When it came to the third verse I had to control myself, it was so funny—'Time is now fleeting, the moments are passing, shadows are gathering, deathbeds are coming, [sic] coming for you and for me.'" (These are anything but the standard, pious words of the hymn; I think they must have sprung from Mom's personal gallows humor.)

In the spring of 1999, when she was almost ninety-two, Mom's health began to fail. In June she suffered an "event," probably a stroke; by that time she was in the nursing wing of her retirement home. The next day, weak and hardly able to walk, she told Judy the word for how she felt was "miserable." And that she did not want to "come back."

Listening to Judy's report, I thought, *Poor Mom. Of course, she doesn't.* I hated to pray for her to die but I did, feeling a strange empathy. *She's ready to go, I've seen it. How awful for someone so energetic and purposeful to feel utterly unable, and not go where she wants when she wants. I hope she doesn't linger.* A few days later, my prayers were answered.

When my daughter Katherine heard of Mom's death, her first reaction was "Oh, no—no more blueberry pies!" Immediately she felt embarrassed, as though she had cared for her grandmother only selfishly or childishly. But Mom would have been delighted, I assured her. Such genuine appreciation, so spontaneously felt! How I wish Mom could have heard that posthumous compliment.

I have found it easy to think of Mom in connection with the blueberries, given their presence in the woods nearby and their significance in cottage life. Mom prized them; after all, she and Dad nurtured those bushes over the years. So many times, I watched her fingers picking over the tiny little berries on a cookie sheet. Andy and I kept on hearing reports of the Thanksgiving and Christmas pies.

Fully ripe, blueberries exhibit a cloudy whitish cast which is a delicate layer of wild yeast known as "bloom." Using the definition of yeast as "an agent of ferment and activity," Mom was indeed the yeast of Craigville.

Yet you had to somehow moderate the intensity of those berries; wild berries are sour indeed, and you do not eat them just for pleasure. They have to be combined with pie crust or batter—and sugar.

Like Mom, with her unquenchable flavor and tartness. Interacting with her, at times it was as though I had gotten a bite with no sugar, perhaps even some leaves and twigs thrown in. Hers was an unfiltered personality. I might have culled some of the berries she put into those pies, but who is to say they were not worthy, perhaps even the best ones? The ones that with cooking, with sugar treatment, held the sharpest, most vivid tastes.

Remembering the pies, and Mom, I press the tip of my tongue against the roof of my mouth, as though I could summon up that dark blue flavor once more.

I am taking a valedictory tone here, something I found myself doing even before Mom died. Even with the problems she posed, I found myself realizing that she was one of the great characters of my life. I wrote about her, though I shared a 1995 essay with only a dear friend; the same for a brief reminiscence of my stay at the cottage with Mom and Pete in 1998.

Even as I found Mom difficult, I kept going to Craigville. I could have refused, I suppose, but I felt I had no choice. Not only was I going to Cape Cod to see my own mother, and that place I loved, but also I was loyal and so was Andy. Besides, even with the difficulties she posed, Mom was fascinating.

Sometimes I think that deep down, I loved Mom to have stayed the course as I did; other times I tell myself, do not sugarcoat her. She was a strong, difficult, un-ignorable, endlessly fascinating woman, and I still stand in awe of her intensity. The polar opposite of someone who "takes things as they come," she engaged with life wholeheartedly, every day. In her last couple of years, she talked a great deal, sometimes way too much. Yet I respected her. From my journal, "If I judged by the detail in which she analyzes and experiences everything, Mom lives as fully, or more so, than anyone else I have ever known."

Underneath it all, I have to admit a sense of not wanting to let Mom get the better of me. Not only did I still not want to concede "the mother-in-law thing" I had been warned of, but I also did not want to acknowledge failure or give up. So always with a multi-month California breather, I kept going back. I had to keep trying. I could hold on, too. A certain defiance has prevailed in my thoughts for many years now.

I will probably never stop trying to understand her. Mom gave such mixed and confounding impressions, was so funny and energetic, so infuriating—and I learned so much from her. In those final years, Mom had to contend mightily with aging, especially the torment of hearing loss; she refused to concede or bow under. Also, she made a major effort not to complain.

Without her, however, I was free. Now I could open the cottage windows and let change blow in.

STAYING ON

*J*uly 1999, a few weeks after Mom's death. The cottage felt dismal. Newspaper obituaries lay on the dining table and possessions from her off-Cape apartment were scattered everywhere: boxes of books, an album of pictures from Andy and my wedding, and piles of pans and dishes on the kitchen table and counters. Like tired soldiers awaiting orders, Mom's cookbooks stood waiting in plastic bags. Everything looked shabby.

I came across a photo album that Mom had made of her Midwest forbears, with labeled photos and portraits from just the era I love to buy in antique shops. *I never knew Mom had put this together . . . . I wish I could thank her and ask more about these people.*

I started unpacking boxes of books and shoving furniture about, then dusting. Just when I had managed to impose a bit of order, brother-in-law Jim and his son arrived with Mom's two small matching couches, which fit in nicely. However, an old cast-iron doctor's scale also came along and for some reason got plunked down in the living room, blighting the charm of the couches. Far too heavy for me or Pete to move, it grimly held pride of place for several more days.

The entire effect was like the old trick: a tablecloth pulled out from under dishes, food, and glassware, leaving them standing. Like the dishes and stemware, all of us, and the cottage, were still standing . . . but Mom's energy was missing.

Or was it? One night soon after, at dinner over at Jim's and Judy's, we were telling stories about her when Jim nudged me and pointed to the box containing her ashes. "Do you think she's listening?"

I wrote in my journal, "I will be so happy to get home . . . to escape the shadow of Mom. I am having such trouble mourning her . . . . I think we were two strong women who could not successfully live together, with all too many layers to complicate the relationship . . . . She was used to controlling—and she had to cope with this independent."

One afternoon, I went with Pete and Andy to a planning session for Mom's memorial service on August 14. To attend, I would have to change my flight; I had not yet decided whether to stay.

The minister who would preside was our old family friend Steve Brown, and we sat on his cool, leafy deck to talk. Choosing the hymns came easily; we all remembered Mom liking *God of Grace* and *God of Glory* and felt equally certain about *O God, Our Help in Ages Past.* Then we talked over scripture passages. For one, Andy volunteered his own musical composition, a psalm setting, with Pete as speaker. We agreed on that, too.

Then someone suggested the famous Old Testament passage about Ruth and Naomi (Ruth 1:8-18). In this story, when Naomi is widowed, as is also Ruth herself, Ruth refuses to leave and pledges her mother-in-law, "Where you go, I will go. Where you lodge, I will lodge. Your people will be my people."

Surprised, I said, "I don't remember Mom having any connection to this story—and I don't see why it fits."

"She often spoke of it," Pete said.

I kept listening to the discussion and wondering. Finally, after I had posed the question once again, he said, "That's how Mom felt about Dad: it expresses her feelings for him."

At that moment, I thought, *I can't do this. I don't want to stay.*

The whole point of this story is loyalty, and I am completely at odds with it. Here I am feeling relieved that I no longer have to contend with

Mom—though I'm thankful that she's no longer ill and suffering. Finally,
I can be myself here . . . I might even relax . . . . I have kept returning and
done my darndest in difficult times, my loyalty has been tested enough . . . .
If I attend that service, someone might apply the story to Mom and me, or
think that this daughter-in-law should make such a vow . . . . People won't
know or care that I helped plan this service, but if they did, would they
think I approved of this passage? . . . I may indeed walk many of the paths
Mom walked, but I am going to find my own way. I have to go home.

On August 14, at the appointed hour, back in California, I held my
own service. I listened to Respighi's *Ancient Airs and Dances for the*
Lute, which Mom had enjoyed so much at a concert that she'd sought
out and sent us a recording. As the music flowed along, I handled
some of her china: the big Japanese antique "flow blue" bowl, plus
her blue-and-white Spode teapot, and two wonderful, contrasting
antique pitchers.

Oh, these pitchers . . . Mom and I talked about them once. The bright
white one is very down home, we agreed, country style, heavy in the hips.
Rustic . . . . To me it calls out for a bunch of daisies . . . . The other pitcher
is very sensual, refined, and ivory rather than white . . . and I love the
curvy lines . . . . Every time I see it, I want to smooth the sides with my
palms . . . . Mom and I agreed that choosing one over the other would be
impossible . . . . Now that I think of it, they seem like two sides of her. It's
too simple to say "the rough and the smooth" but I kept meeting up with
that vehement, opinionated soul versus the friendly, interesting mind I
could just enjoy.

Things were the easy part of Mom's legacy. Her house, the cottage
itself, and later her apartment contained an eclectic mixture of
beautiful objects, antiques, and foreign or primitive things. One wall
in particular presented an almost Smithsonian variety: two painted
Balinese wood panels of dancers next to a Victorian landscape in an
ornate gold-encrusted frame. Alongside these, two carved ivory whales
from Nantucket on a plaque and nearby a pair of commanding wooden
busts of African women with protruding lips, about 20 inches high,

whose expressions always made me feel uneasy. Close by, a framed collection of old political campaign buttons and ribbons.

Mom liked every one. Things offered common ground: if we both responded to an object, it was a point of friendly talk between us.

As I thought about them all, I began to talk to Mom. I confessed that I still held anger. Anger that I had had to conform to her, to fit into that lifestyle, and not expect her to be much interested in my passions. Above all, I felt angry that so much had been left unexpressed or unsolved.

"Mom, I guess now that a lot of my anger is going into mourning you. I think you and I were two strong women who could have been friends but were only occasionally. We just lived too far apart, I guess . . . and our viewpoints were so different . . . . I learned so much from you, but I am still puzzled by how you treated me . . . though I do know that one problem is, we were always on each other's turf . . . . Andy and I kept coming back to the cottage so loyally. I do not think I deserved that treatment you handed out . . . and you never apologized or tried to talk anything out or come to some arrangement we could both live with.

"It is terrible to say this, but I am glad to be free of you, Mom. Although I know it will be a lot of work, Andy and I really look forward to being at the cottage now."

The following summer at Craigville, 2000, a heady state of mind took me over. Often, as I planned or carried out some job, the ungracious thought, *I'm free! I can watch the sunset—and damn the dishes!*

I could take care of the dishes, really any domestic work, when I felt its time had come. Better still, I could control my own time. For "watch the sunset," I might also "take a walk in the woods." Do nothing. Think. Read. I could choose not to go on a shopping trip. With no one commenting on my choice, I could sink into the Sunday *New York Times* on the porch on a perfect beach afternoon or go to the beach only for lunch and a quick swim.

Best of all, I could sit down and write whenever I wanted to.

One evening's sunset. "A cerise marvel sky! Bands of green-black trees, then the thick fabric of marsh green and the scraggly border of weeds and bushes below where I sit on the lawn. Grass blades tickle my legs, the air's faintly salty . . . . The marsh has become thick and indistinct now, a lateral green soup. Thankfully, there are few bugs. I hear kids playing somewhere in the village. Their voices sound rather like forks and knives clinking in soapy water . . . . I'm conscious of a density of dark descending, as if there were some cell of cool, delicious breeze on each pore of my skin."

Another evening. "Out on the porch. The sun's going down behind the point of land across the marsh, silhouetting a leafy filigree of treetops. Below lies a calm expanse of reeds, water, and mud. During these sunset moments, still drawn out even late in August, the light turns rose gold and descends in layers, softly gilding branches and tree trunks on the hillside. A trace of breeze stirs the trees! Leaves and branches weave pattern after pattern, web after web. With each flicker and sway, sunlight reaches through the tiny squares of screen, channeled into facets, almost winking. Faces, dishes, glasses, and even all our mixed-up old furniture are suffused with a rosy glow that lessens ever so slowly. When dusk finally descends, I'm surprised to realize it's dark."

One evening I recorded, "Spent most of the day just being here . . . just for us, just simply enjoying this place that is so potent and beautiful."

But I had hardly taken on a life of sitting and doing nothing. I had to work out a balance between caring for the place and leaving room for my soul. Every day, I would uncover some new detail or impression. "This quirky old house! The furnishings are as random and helter-skelter as the people who've brought them together." I began to wonder, "What's constant here? This building, on this piece of land, owned and populated by this family. Or is the only constant the land itself, and wind and rain, trees and sky and water? . . No, God who created it and all of us—that is the constant."

Even as I tried to clear my mind, Mom's busy spirit haunted the cottage. But when I thought of her sixty years' shaping the place, how could I expect her to have left?

I did control my own thoughts. That is, instead of petulant or angry defiance, I began to figure out what I could learn. *I do not want to act the way she did. I can do better.* Yet this kind of thinking brought some guilt along with it. *Who are you to be so holier than thou—than she? And what a negative way to learn.* However, I decided that I was learning from experience and making something useful of it. And I made some resolutions.

I want people to know that they are valued and loved. I will work at phrasing my thoughts helpfully and constructively; I will express affection.

If I am not getting along with someone, I will apologize. I will try to talk things out. I will acknowledge my part in the problem and work at changing. I will not just shove it all under the rug and then explode, leaving hurt behind with nothing resolved or changed.

For myself, I would also work at daring to write and think. Give myself space and try to miss nothing. I tried to find positive room in my thoughts. One night I wrote, "Thank goodness I don't feel the anger I felt before. Somehow I'm managing to avoid that . . . . Then it was still a current of anger at Mom, at her lingering presence . . . . I've come out from under, I am hardly competing with her anymore."

Oh, really? No, still processing. For several summers, my feelings were in a constant push-pull state. "That tough adamant spirit/person who had Her Ways of Doing Things, which all of us kowtowed to. Many of them are discarded now. Mom set the tone, one lacking affirmation or affection (except for little children), and often tolerance. I think she did love us in her way, but boy, it was a tough and seldom reassuring way."

"I can act here now, not always react to Mom . . . . I am really living here, instead of being a visitor."

But it was one thing to declare something, another to keep acting with a new spirit. I had also taken on a busy life. One evening in 2002

I wrote, "Here I am, grumping about, and not making any particular sense. At times it seems as if that's what this place does to me—I love it here but my mind splits into hundreds of jigsaw puzzle pieces and seldom do they fit together, even two or three of them."

Every day I was doing many of the same things Mom had done; sitting in her chair, the cook's position closest to the kitchen, I dispensed English muffins from the toaster with the old tongs; as she had done, I sometimes dashed off to the supermarket before breakfast, before the place got busy. As Mom must have done hundreds of times, I made beds and put out towels. Ran load after load of laundry.

I also wrote, "Mom would not have done what I'm doing now, 10 a.m.: this would be housecleaning or organized group activity time— and I'm sitting here writing." I was getting things down on paper, preaching to myself, cheering myself on, and asking questions.

Much of the time, Mom might not have seen herself as dominating matters or intending to do so. But her forcefulness, her vehemence of speech, often flattened me, especially the sense, intended or not, that "All thinking people would naturally agree with what I say." That forcefulness put her words in bold type and added almost a sense of threat to some of her acts. Over time, she came through as though saying, "Listen to me! Take my words and thoughts and absorb them and act on them. I'm the one who knows, who's got the truth—or the important ideas—on her side." The one who dares to be in charge.

Perhaps competition between us had been inevitable.

DOMAIN

*O*ne evening I wrote in my journal, "I feel the silence, feel a sense of calm—it's needed, yet it's a little unnatural for this house. Does this somehow speak of lessened vitality, or some past happenings suppressed? There's space for me now, fewer people, more peace . . . though I feel a price has been paid . . . . Now I can think. And cook, entertain, and enjoy people in ways I never have before."

I began to feel some sense of personal domain, starting with finding yet more charming Victorian dishes and glassware in the pantry to serve with, or learning which bushes and shrubs in the yard furnished the best greenery for bouquets. I brightened up the place with new tablecloths and local pottery. At home in California, I would start planning meals and earmark or photocopy recipes; once at Craigville, how satisfying it was to have the whole family over for supper, especially to invite back in one of our nephews whom Mom had pretty much banished. I could get to know people in the village, too, including some who had never before set foot in our cottage and were curious. In addition to maintaining the family's long-standing Craigville relationships, I began to make friends of my own and went out for lunch or coffee with them.

I also began to travel to Craigville in memory. Once I got myself through a lengthy dental procedure by mentally touring the cottage;

during a nasty spell of drilling, I went "out on the porch" to take in the view, thinking wistfully of a cool gin and tonic. This led to musing over the pegboard in the kitchen. *All those old utensils, now just what hangs where? Strainers, measuring cups, and . . . those bumpy-bottomed old saucepans that hang from holes in the handles . . . oh, and all the stuff on the pantry shelves by the window.* Here my practical self kicked in, as I knew Pete and others would already have occupied the cottage. *What on earth am I to do with all those huge cans of beans I know I will find? And surely some vegetable that we have entirely too much of, aging away in the veggie bin . . . . On the other hand, I can buy wonderful scallops and swordfish back there! Really fresh . . . . Oh, and if Carl and Kathy come, we'll have their incredible tomatoes again. Ahh . . . I'll lay them out on the old Limoges platter, red, orange, and yellow slices, and even that heirloom variety with the odd greenish red color and weird bulbous shapes—they're the real thing if I ever met up with it . . . .*

Yet as always, I was also living with the family network: the Buffingtons sprang into action. Other people had ideas, too. Niece Jo and her husband Dean, who came at different times from us, worked like Trojans, painting and freshening the place up. Andy and Pete soon undertook some major modernizing steps the cottage needed, which had been impossible to carry out in Mom's final years. However, I found it hard to live with the guys' paranoia about town regulations: The Broze knew what should be done, always with loud talk and speculation. More than once, I thought, *For goodness sakes! I could make these decisions and plans without all this fuss and still do it rationally and clearly. Faster, too.*

One day Andy said to me, half joking, "What's a nice girl like you doing in a place like this?"

I sometimes wondered. I was living in a place where it often seemed that nothing happened in any sort of order: life was a jumble, starting with the pantry. "So many dishes, so many sizes and shapes! Serving a meal here, you can dress food in several different costumes . . . . I always find something perfectly suited . . . . Hmm . . . I can serve up ideas in all shapes and sizes, too."

The earthy side. "I know who's in the next room by the sound of the burps . . . . This is a place where people sit on the toilet with the bathroom door open and discuss the paint job they're doing."

Home repairs. One afternoon Andy brought me out to show off progress on rebuilding the back porch, saying, "Plenty of talk's gone into this!" *I have no trouble believing that.*

Pete added, "It's sort of a Dylan Thomas extended poem sometimes . . . ."

One morning, seven o'clock. "The cottages across the river look sleepy, like roosting birds reflected in the water. The scene's a luminist painting. Just outside the porch where I'm sitting, no leaves are stirring, yet the nearest tree looks arrested in mid-dance, its trunk and branches dark, the light behind—as though it were frozen in the old kids' game of Statues."

Sunset. "It's fascinating the way nature's time affects our dinners on the porch . . . something about the lengthening sun and early evening hours. Sitting out there, the main course more or less done, people pull their chairs back, still sipping wine. Talk winds down a bit, then is lazily picked up again. It's as though the long rays loosen and stretch out our thinking, and every chair invisibly reclines into a chaise longue. As the sunlight diminishes, it softens and somehow warms every object, every face, and makes it self-luminous."

Always the thought: "Oh, there is so much to try to hold here! And about one ten-thousandth of the time I need to do it."

Then the summer of 2003: a major life event took over, the marriage of our older daughter Katherine. Though I did not realize it then, playing my part in the whole affair gave me a place at Craigville.

Although Katherine was not, as the old phrase has it, "married from the house"—the wedding and reception took place at a conference center nearby—we had lots of people on hand to cook for, or at least arrange for food to appear. We made myriad runs to the bus station and grocery store, did laundry, made beds, took phone calls, and carried out unexpected arrangements of all kinds.

Katherine and I arrived early in July. On the fifth, I wrote, "A sweet wind is gently brushing about and causing millions of leaves to turn and shimmer in the sun . . . swish, swish." Out on the porch, over coffee, she and I made a long list of jobs. From then on, every day brought meetings with caterer or photographer or someone else necessary; I kept all the resulting papers in a big loose-leaf. One day I recorded, ". . . good thing I'm a fairly proficient organizer."

Other details. "The faintest air of cool breeze is moving the curtains like languid fingers." Or the night Andy arrived. "His grand and wonderful for-me smile is as handsome as ever."

Though the wedding gown had been ordered the summer before, only now could we take delivery. And "delivery" was the word for the day Katherine, Andy, and I went to pick it up. The salon owner had broken her arm, so instead of watching her stage the great try-on, I found myself helping my daughter.

Though larger than normal fitting rooms, this one was an intimate space, soft pink, carpeted, cushioned, and curtained. With my hands holding the bodice, Katherine bowed her head, arms, and upper torso into the gown. Momentarily, both of us were enveloped in and connected by layers and layers of sumptuous, heavy fabric. Then, as the dress shifted from my hands onto her body, I thought, *It's almost as though I'm giving birth to her again.* Smiling into the mirror, she straightened up and I went to work fastening her in—and there she stood, reborn as a bride. Beautiful!

Once home, she and I carried the gown in its pink plastic bag upstairs and laid it on the extra bed in her room. That evening I recorded, "The gown is as lovely as we remembered! We should have had the photographer with us to catch all K's delighted expressions."

The next morning, catching a glimpse as I passed the partially open door, I almost said, "Well, hello! Whose body is this? Did you just get here?"

Yet a little while later, I went in to wake Katherine herself and thought, *When she's asleep, she still looks like a little girl. . . .*

Soon the groom arrived. "I watch David working at fitting in, trying as I did long ago, to make sense of the Buffingtons at Craigville." We welcomed him with a family dinner on the porch, including a ritual Scotch tasting set out by Pete. Judy and Jim came, bringing part of dinner. It was one of those magnificent special evenings: I later noted "that place, that wonderful time. This family in its house, its treasure place . . . ."

Still, I kept scribbling. "Much is in place but mental walk-throughs are now in order, as is the ability to recognize what's missing or hadn't been thought of—I seem to be fairly good at this." A couple of nights later, 2 a.m. "I come downstairs, get a glass of milk, trying to de-muddle myself . . . . I feel buzzy, fragmented." A few days later. "I am bombarded by thoughts and 'Oh, I forgots' as thickly as though I were walking within a swarm of insects."

Two nights before The Wedding. More people arrived, the musicians bickered and rehearsed, details and phone calls multiplied, and every bedroom was occupied. My big loose-leaf continued to serve.

That Thursday night, I served dinner to a swarm of people, including most of the bridal party and David's family from Nova Scotia. Seventeen of us ranged all over the house and porches.

The wedding day! The tent the caterer had urged us to rent proved its worth when a five-minute shower fell right before the ceremony. Then the sky cleared and thank goodness, stayed clear. Everything worked, the wedding spun out . . . reunions, embraces . . . welcomes and goodbyes . . . . At the reception, dancing and a most wonderful surprise: the groom and groomsmen lined up, arm in arm, and sang Stan Rogers' songs from Nova Scotia. Then Katherine and David took off—and it was all over.

Or was it?

About eleven that night, I went upstairs, kicked off my shoes, put on a more comfortable dress, and lay down on the bed with a five-minute rest in mind—and awoke the next morning. That afternoon we all went to the beach and got silly and threw seaweed at each other. Katherine's friend Lisa had the right take on that: "It's stress relief time at the Buffingtons'!" Another relief was being taken out to dinner that evening by Pete, an odd occasion indeed with all the women high as kites and the men uncharacteristically silent, dog tired.

Having had no time to record anything for several days, on Monday I wrote down every single thing I could remember, ending up with five pages of names and phrases. Also questions. "What to do with the leftovers from the caterers?" (Eat them up the next night.) "We realized that you don't need sixty invitations for sixty guests." (No solution to that one.) I listed, "What I did well, and what I didn't." Also, "I am just plain worn out."

With rest and several days of porch time, however, I regained myself. The house settled back down, too. Now only Pete, Andy, and I held the fort and a wave of wedding euphoria settled over the three of us.

However, a few days later, a local newspaper published an article about the village of Craigville, with the headline "Residents Cherish Serenity of Historic Cottage Colony."

Serenity? What was that? Of course, I had to concede that any wedding, unless extremely small, complicates life. But I could not help thinking, too, how this family I had married into lived a complex cottage existence all the time. Serenity? Tranquility? Oh, no.

Musing, I wrote, "Busyness is what distinguishes this family . . . . None of us can imagine it otherwise . . . . We all just engage, wherever we are, in a grand, verbose thrash-it-all-out sort of life, and we keep coming here and taking up this humming sort of life and that's who we are. Life here is a whole 'nother life—I have long known it is no vacation." Tennyson's phrase "Life piled on life" (from *Ulysses*) describes the Buffingtons well.

And me. For I began to think being at the cottage was a spur to creativity and thinking. My mind and emotions got so stimulated and I was forced to consider many options, a different bunch of viewpoints, and surroundings. I wrote, "I cannot sink into too much of a groove in California because I know I will have to shift back here every year and put that real life behind me . . . . Yet I am real here, too."

But eventually, I might not shift thinking at all, instead just bounce back from one well-known place to another, like alternating between two sets of clothes. What had been Mom's take on this double-existence idea? She had lived it, too, though with far less physical distance between the two locations.

Just as I had helped my daughter into the wedding gown, birthing her into another stage of life, that summer I had brought the cottage into its next generation. The wedding had offered me a conventional role to play—and I had done it well. An arranger like Mom, and a competent one at that, but also a friendly, accommodating, and nurturing presence, I had officially set out the domestic landscape as it would be now and for the coming years.

Now I could birth my own creative life there. How would I carry this out?

DESK

To begin with, where would I write? Other than any place that happened to be quiet at the moment. Not only did upstairs often get hot, but also our bedroom wasn't large and Andy frequently went to bed before I did. And the only desk in the cottage was smack in the middle of the living room: Ground Zero, the junction of voices and stair steps, comings and goings.

Seeing the desk, you'd probably say, "That's a nice old piece!" Slant-topped, probably manufactured in the 1930s or '40s, it was made of maple, though the warm reddish brown looked more like what I think of as "cherry," a hue like oak leaves in the fall. Below the pull-down writing surface were three deep, wide drawers, each with two simple brass handles. When you opened up the desk, five arched cubbyholes revealed themselves at the back, as well as a shallow drawer beneath each cubby. The writing surface usually featured tape, pads, paper clips, pens, and snapshots, also a blotter.

After Dad died, the desk became pretty much Mom's, appropriately enough, though we all dipped in occasionally for tape or scissors. I never felt welcome beyond that, though. To me, a desk came with space around it, even a room: private space. Something there had never been much of in the cottage. For years, I had managed without, knowing that my visits would be short.

Eventually, however, that communal desk became the nucleus of my "room of one's own." And "eventually" translated into a process that took place over several summers, involving not just my wish for a place to work and write, but the family situation I had grown up with.

Ever since I had been old enough to notice what goes with or in a house, I had considered a personal desk a necessary piece of equipment: a house for the mind. I had grown up revering my mother's polished mahogany slant-top desk. Full of compartments and little drawers, with elegant brass hardware, it appeared polite and socially graceful. She kept it in beautiful order. By contrast, my father organized his life in multi-drawered office desks. Flat and table-like, they conveyed both business efficiency and a sense of taming life, keeping his concerns— and some personal items—in neat piles, also in well-kept file cabinets. Acquiring my own maple student desk was a milestone in my growing-up years; I took it as a sign of coming adulthood.

Later, I became even more idealistic: a desk as a visible cave dwelling for thought that gives an outward and visible sign of inward, even spiritual, churning and work over time. A desk acts as the gondola of a mental balloon yet is also the place where I come back down to earth, and a nest. At the same time, it is an interesting object in and of itself. A desk says, this person has taken charge of life here. It registers that you have decided you live in this place: here is your *locus in quo*.

And I had taken these ideas one step further: a desk is where the writer resides.

Not only was the cottage desk located in the living room, but also a commonly public piece of furniture, an upright piano, resided in the downstairs bedroom. At least in daytime, this was all right for someone playing solo; though duets were possible, for any larger group of people, sharing music in there was impossible.

A year or two after Mom died, watching our dear friend Carl, a fine oboist, perched on the edge of the saggy bed to play Bach sonatas with Andy at the piano, I thought, *This arrangement is not just awkward, it's crazy.*

I spoke up. "Hey, guys, let's move the piano into the living room and put the desk in the bedroom! Then you can easily play with Carl,

Andy, and we can play trios or quartets, even, that way, too . . . . Oh, and maybe we could take out the old twin beds and put a sofa bed in the bedroom to open up space—and that would offer a good place to get away from the TV if you don't want to watch in the evening."

Andy considered. "Well, you know, that room's always been a crummy place for the piano. I've never understood how it got put there."

Furrowing his brow, Pete said, "You just might have a point. Let's think it over."

After a few days of discussion, we exchanged piano and desk. Now people could play chamber music in a room with better acoustics, more space, and no one traipsing through on the way to the bathroom. Also, the piano itself, with its handsome Victorian panels of carved leaf designs, could be seen to advantage. Back in the bedroom, the new sofa bed created not only quarters for guests needing a place with no stairs and a private bath, but also, most of the time, a lovely reading corner.

However, though the move helped others, I was the prime beneficiary of the desk's new home. Up to that time, I had always schlepped around my notebooks and papers, usually leaving them in a corner at the back of the living room. I worried little about anyone reading my stuff; the cottage had always seemed like a summer camp where individual pursuits were hardly noticed. But as writing became more and more vital to me, and my stays grew longer, I had come to need privacy and quiet.

Problem solved.

Or was it?

Both the desk and the room it now occupied had been Mom's. Clearing out the desk after she died, I'd found her old checkbook ledgers, papers and letters, poignant reminders of her long friendships, as well as her stash of cards for many occasions and her address book. Seeing them all, I felt as though Mom's flowing, idiosyncratic handwriting had somehow inscribed the entire piece of furniture; all her above- and below-the-line tails of g's and f's had invisibly reached out like quivering tendrils into the cubby holes. So invested with her personality was it, the desk's "Lois-ness" threatened to expand and fill the whole room.

My confidence wavered. Should I use this desk at all? Let alone sit in her room to write.

On a first try, I felt almost illicit. Besides, even if I did claim the desk, should we need that room and its sofa bed for guests, I knew I would be displaced.

Still, the real issue was that the desk had been Mom's and the room had been hers. Alice Brown, an understanding Craigville friend who had known Mom, suggested, only half-kidding, that I hold an exorcism so I would feel free to make my claim. I never did, though musing on Alice's idea helped.

Over a couple more summers, I moved into the idea, that is, the desk. But not without preparing my way. On our last day in September 2003, I stood on the front walk, suitcase in hand, taking one last look around at the house before we flew home and left the cottage to its long winter sleep. Andy was locking up.

Facing the house, looking in the direction of the desk, I muttered, "Mom, course around all you want. The house is yours . . . for now. See you next summer! But when I come back, I am writing in that room. I'm taking over."

Ever since, I have worked at the desk. I use tools Mom never had: laptop, printer, and digital camera. Every summer I install a table alongside for these and my personal papers, trying (seldom successfully) to keep the main surface clear for others. Soon, Pete took to calling the room my office.

I sit at the desk probably longer and more often than Mom ever did; I love the views of trees and marsh out the windows on either side. As the desk sits in the corner of not only the room but also the house, when I work, I turn my back on the family. With time, the room has come to mean for me the desk, even the mind of the house. Here is prime space where I think and remember, take notes, and make inner connections: my corner.

AFOOT

*A*nd how about the world around me at Craigville? It was time to get outdoors and walk and explore.

Of course, I had gone out before. But most of the time, such activity—blueberry picking, hanging wash on the clothesline, watching the kids, or lining up on the front porch for a family picture——had been limited, in a group, or suggested by somebody else.

I needed to learn this place for itself, and for myself.

In this desire, I was returning to how I had lived my teen years on Cape Cod, when I walked nearly every day over my family's three acres. Whatever the season, I left the house and went either to the sandy beach on the pond, or around the scrub pines and oaks sheltering our cottages, or along the paths on the hillsides overlooking the water. All summer I swam, often several times a day, and in winter I skated, though my joy in that freedom became only a memory after the day the ice gave under me. The other three seasons of the year, I rowed all over that pond, throwing my whole body into the job of propelling myself.

Summers always involved a private ritual: toughening up winter-tender feet so I could go barefoot and feel in touch with the place. No one imposed this requirement on me, it just became a point of honor. I just kept walking and walking until I could go anywhere without hesitation.

Now Craigville's woods and paths lay ahead, so one morning I set out to make a circumnavigation akin to walking the bounds, that early English tradition in which one walks a parcel of land or a parish to take stock of condition and property lines. I would walk my way into knowing this place via skin and sense and thought.

From the front step, I padded over the lawn, dodging twigs and pinecones among the grass blades; then I rounded the corner of the porch, went down the gentle slope below, and took a path bordered with cheerful clumps of grass and weeds. Its packed dirt was interspersed with pine needles, dry leaves, twigs, and tooth-sized pebbles: familiar Cape Cod ground.

When I reached the back yard, the path turned to concrete, seventy-five-year-old concrete, that is. Pebbly and grainy, it felt anything but smooth, though the soles of my feet enjoyed its coolness. However, over the years the sections had gotten heaved up so a plate here did not quite meet a plate there. All those tips and slopes made for interesting walking, like conversations that keep veering off subject, something which often happened in the cottage. Suddenly tilting, I almost lost my balance and was reminded of walking aboard ship, as though the cottage were a great ark overlooking the salt marsh. Correcting course, I went on, vowing to stop only where and when I wanted to.

And here was the marsh! Acres and acres of muddy, buggy ground, home to herons, ospreys, ducks, fish, and crabs. Foxes and coons beat paths across; thousands of wood ticks dwelt there, too. As kids, Andy and his brothers used to catch blue crabs there and take day trips in a rowboat down the tidal river that runs through. Officially termed a wetland, to me the marsh is sacred ground. Basic Cape Cod, wild, open land largely without people.

I stopped and let my eyes roam. Instead of rushed glimpses as I hung up laundry or emptied the compost, I could gaze out over the marsh as long as I wanted. How high was the tide right now? Was that a heron out there poking in the mud? Wind and bird calls and the hum of lawnmowers and trucks' backup beeps and children's voices—all combined into an outdoor music. Yet another mix of sensations, I inhaled: a combo of sun on grass, salt air, and marsh mud.

Turning around, I looked up at the cottage; from here I could see its full three stories looming. Then, dodging flapping sheets and towels, I padded over scrappy grass under the clotheslines and headed past the kitchen steps. Another turn. Yet more concrete, some of it a flat path, and leading off to my left, a sloping walkway with old-fashioned urn-shaped corner planters. Ahead, a flight of wooden steps led to the open porch on the east side, where the cottage overlooked the road and village. Andy's grandparents used to consider that section the most pleasant of all. Come afternoon, it would be shady and cool, but their descendants seldom used it.

Going along below the porch, I turned once more and walked forward to the front steps, where I had so often joined family photos, taken first sightings of the day's weather, called people to the phone, or welcomed visitors.

To mark the end point of my journey, I stood still, took a breath, and engaged in *tadasana*, the yoga pose known as the mountain. Positioning the soles of my feet flat on the ground, I centered myself and aligned my entire body; finally, I extended my arms upward. Complete. I had made the circuit, the rounds. In the process, I had raised my focus from physical ground to the terrain of mind and heart—yet now I encompassed both, a metaphor for how I operated at the cottage. How I operate anywhere. Borrowing a term from Thoreau, I was fully "a sojourner in civilized life"—and still a barefoot self.

Done with my walk, I then went in and sat down to write about my morning. Just as my body had matured from that of the barefoot teenager, I sought to go deeper now. As though not only my feet were bare, but also the rest of me.

THE NEXT PIE

*F*our o'clock, back from the beach. Into the kitchen: time to get dinner together! Andy's brother Jim and his wife Judy were coming.

Unwrapping a pre-cut circle of pastry and nesting it in a dish, I was visited with a memory of Mom making pie crust on the white enamel table. I could just see her: flattening and then rolling out a ball of dough into a circle, then manipulating it expertly. Brow furrowed in concentration, she would crimp the edges with her fingertips, just so.

As I stood at the counter and trimmed off extra flaps of pastry with a paring knife, I almost felt her watching.

Who's cooking here, Mom, you or me?

Now to assemble the filling. I took two baskets of strawberries from the fridge. Oh, no, what crummy berries! Not very many left, either. *I just bought these yesterday.* With much hulling, trimming, and slicing, I managed to salvage a scant cup and a half. *Thank goodness they don't have to be perfectly shaped inside a pie.* On to the rhubarb. Pulling stalks out of a plastic bag, I found a whole lot of decaying brown ends. Another salvage job. Chop, chop, trim! I added the rhubarb to the berries in a big measuring cup. Barely four cups of fruit—and I needed six.

Oh, hell. Now what?

Did I have time to scoot to the supermarket? Nope. Besides, a glance out the window told me the car was gone.

So, as Mom must also have done, I looked to see what else we had on hand. Hmm, apples. *Well, they'll do to fill things out—and apples blend in. Nobody will know the difference.* Further peeling and slicing brought the fruit up to five and a half cups. I stirred and added sugar. But now the proportions looked wrong: not enough berries.

I rummaged in the fridge again. Strawberry jam? *Wow, that's awfully sweet, but I don't see any other option.* I scooped up a good-sized gob and mixed it in with the fruit. *Sure improves the color.* Grabbing a lemon, I cut a hefty section and squeezed in the juice. *Lemon will perk up anything.* Stir again. Then I dumped all the fruit into the pie shell and smoothed it down with the back of a spoon.

Now to unfurl the second crust . . . oh, how about twisted latticework? That would be pretty. Gingerly cutting and curling the strips, I loop-de-looped the pastry across the top. Aha! *Easier than I had thought, how nice.* I sealed and crimped the edges, sprinkled cinnamon sugar over the whole thing, took one last appraising look, and shoved it in the oven. *Not bad, Sally!*

Later, just as I took out the pie, Jim came into the kitchen to refill gin-and-tonics.

"Wow! Is that for dessert? It looks wonderful and it smells delicious!"

"Yes, doesn't it?" *But handsome is as handsome tastes. I bet Mom would have thought so, too.*

When I brought the pie to the table and started to serve, crimson juices bubbled up in the diamond-shaped gaps between strips of crust. Someone said, "That looks like Martha Stewart made it!" We all inhaled a fruity perfume, then forks clinked on plates.

"Oh, Sally, this is marvelous!" This from Judy, herself a fine cook. High praise indeed.

Now I tasted, too . . . aah! Good. *Now that's what strawberry-rhubarb pie should taste like . . . and they're asking for seconds . . . . Oh my gosh, it's all gone!*

No, it was not a blueberry pie, that cottage specialty. Also, "from scratch" had translated into a good deal of scrabbling around to manage something good. For quite a while afterward, I privately referred to that strawberry-rhubarb job as The Impossible Pie. In my own eyes at least, I had equaled Mom at the pie game, because along with a fair amount of luck, that pie contained a large measure of competitiveness. Cue in Sinatra singing *My Way*. That pie was a poster child for my culinary independence—and inventiveness.

"Impossible?" Of course not. I often improvise in the kitchen; Mom did, too. You have to. And such creations have been known to produce lots of good things. Once when I made carrot-ginger soup to use up too many bags of carrots bought on special, I basked in Pete's reaction: "There's nothing like a good soup." Also, I have always loved designing menus and especially enjoy making up recipes as I go along. *What will I make with the peaches? . . . . Oh, and those tomatoes ripening on the windowsill . . . stuff them? Or simply serve them sliced with cukes and red onions?* My eyes trace the shapes as I muse. Such thinking is all part of a style of cooking one might describe as "Take this bunch of stuff on hand and see what you can make of it." I have never forgotten a marvelous chocolate bread pudding Mom once made to use up stale bread one evening long ago. Then, too, I remember an apple crisp I was once served with crushed potato chips on top, desperate improvising gone over the edge.

We all try to live by the old adage: *Use it up, wear it out, make it do, do without.*

Another sign of my newfound cottage independence was sitting in Mom's place at the end of the table close to the kitchen, the place where I felt (at least somewhat) in control of things. For cooking and managing the kitchen meant respect and a major position in the way things worked. The cottage was a stimulating place to cook, too, though I sometimes had to field such comments as "This chicken—or turkey or tuna or whatever it is—is very good."

All together, I was finding cottage cooking something of a test: all those food preferences and tastes. With vegetarians, meatatarians, athletic health food types, vegans, small children, and potato chip junkies on board, shopping trips were scenes of complex negotiation. After one expedition, I felt as though I had been to a square dance where all the sets had gotten tangled up.

Most of the time the poor fridge was like a hotel full of pushy and ever-changing guests. As chef, you were both desk clerk and manager; someone had to keep things organized. And all too often, Murphy's Law came to dinner. Whatever you served, somebody would not like some part of it or was allergic to it, plus Murphy usually—no, always— arrived at the last minute.

Yet as cook, I was the backbone of the family, a sense reaffirmed for me one summer evening when we visited friends. I had contributed a sliced veggie salad, a bakery pie, and wine; they served barbecued chicken and corn on the cob. After dinner, our host Nevin, then in his late eighties, pointed to a large white tureen on the sideboard, saying, "That was Elizabeth's favorite serving dish. She liked to do chicken a la king in it for a party. She made that a lot—it was good!—and she liked to have people come and eat and have a good time. She liked making it happen."

I knew exactly what he meant. For I, too, love "making it happen." So did Mom. The role of producer, of giver. When I cook, I think about who I am serving. I love how pleased people look when something good is put on the table, and how our son-in-law once inhaled the aroma of spaghetti and meatballs, motioning the steam toward his face as though it were manna from Heaven. I feel happy seeing family cars draw up down below the cottage when I've just taken a pan of lasagna out of the oven. All these things give me a feeling of mothering and the sense that if I did not bring all this together, who would?

Food is elemental: food tells me I am home. And even though I worked in that kitchen for only a few weeks each summer, cooking was a major way I lived at the cottage. Cooking made me a member of the family—and when I sliced, baked, sautéed, and brought together the meals we shared, I served the elements of communion.

THE BROZE

*I*n my early years at Craigville, I often felt like a little girl thrown in among the big boys at the playground. The brothers gesticulated and popped with ideas as they discussed politics, gossiped, and conducted investigations into the origins and costs of prized objects. Talk, jokes, stories, and reports on *New Yorker* articles flashed by in rapid succession. Everything, food included, got digested verbally.

Although I did not cotton to this meaning back then, a joke one night at dinner could have been told to show me my place, though I doubt it was meant for the purpose.

Imagine a jail or some other kind of closed community where all the jokes have been told so many times that no one bothers any longer to actually tell a story. Instead, someone calls out, "Number Twenty-seven!" Everybody laughs.

Another voice: "Okay, Number Thirteen!"

Hearty guffaws and chortles.

One day, however, a new inmate arrives who listens and takes it all in. Finally getting up his courage, he calls out, "Number Twenty-two!"

Except for the newbie's nervous chuckle, complete silence.

Surprised, he says, "Why didn't anyone laugh? I don't get it."

"Oh, it's all in the telling!"

Such a thing is perhaps inevitable in any family, but telling was especially prominent at Craigville. The Buffingtons had Family Stories and a lot more of them, proudly repeated and often discussed, than my own family ever did. Even without Mom, staying at Craigville meant living with voluble and forthcoming people who loved to talk: the Broze.

After my initial dazzlement, I learned to speak up. But with my 1993 essay I had not only announced that I was serious about writing, I also began to speak out more. I challenged some assumptions and started to act more strongly on my own behalf. Analyzing what played out in front of me, I wanted to be the one telling stories—on paper, anyway—and I was working to learn how.

One step I took was to attend summer writing workshops including *Memoir: The Self in Society*, taught by Marc Nieson, at the Iowa Summer Writing Festival. The twelve of us students read, discussed, and critiqued each other's essays. We looked at our lives and analyzed our families, also old photographs, and discussed examples of published writing. Everyone shared freely yet listened well, too. Marc Nieson was (and I am sure still is) an informed and talented mentor whose personality set the tone; he inspired me greatly. Not only did I return home with a long reading list and work to do, I also received a heady feeling of being myself, as though I, via my writing and thinking, were—or might become—a jewel in a setting.

A few weeks later, I flew to Craigville as usual for several weeks with Andy and Pete. Looking back now, I think of that summer (and every summer since) as two workshops I was to keep on attending. By myself, writing, I was a self who worked to understand her relationship with and place in society; at Craigville, I kept living out an ongoing tale: *Sally and The Broze*.

Could only two people constitute a society? Yes, when they were Andy and Pete, a subset of the Buffington brothers. Sometimes oldest brother Jim would join us, too, and on one of those occasions I began to call them The Broze: a group of quirky, talkative guys with whom I was connected and whose words and actions often (to use an old phrase of my father's) "gave me furiously to think."

One instance, an evening at Craigville. Pete was sitting at the table sorting through some personal financial stuff. Reading on my own, I paid no attention until I heard paper ripping. I glanced over to see Pete tearing apart little papers (credit card receipts, I think) with his teeth and muttering, "All I need is animal fat to become a Sepoy!"

"What on earth are you talking about?"

Oldest brother Jim, who happened to be listening—quick, jam in the answer first!—explained that this related to the Sepoy Rebellion of 1850 against the British in India. Soldiers used some kind of ammunition which had to be torn open with the teeth, then sealed with animal fat.

The things these guys know . . . I had heard of the Sepoy Rebellion but couldn't have named its date, nor would I ever have dreamed that some fact about it would be relevant to people I knew and what they did.

That was a very Broze moment, with all the characteristic elements: delight in facts, one-upmanship, reference to history (the more esoteric the better), and the way some mundane thing became grander as a result of such an explanation.

I thanked Jim and asked, "That's unusual stuff; where did you ever learn it?"

This time, Pete shot first. "Oh, at Exeter, one of the history courses." Referring to Phillips Exeter, the New Hampshire prep school all three had attended.

Calling the guys "the Broze" was suggested by Jim, though he offered the moniker as a joke. It came about like this. Andy and I had won the bidding at a church auction for a week at a cottage on Nantucket Island (south of Cape Cod), so we invited the family to join us there for the first non-Craigville reunion ever. As I prepared for the trip that October, I thought, *Oh, now's my chance! I can observe these guys in a new place, someone else's cottage with no repairs to do—all they have to do is be themselves together, as though I've cast them in a sitcom.*

We had a great time, though the island was chilly and austere in that season—and beautiful. As usual, I kept a journal. Noticing me scribbling one evening, Jim glanced over and said, "Hey, Sally, I bet you're storing up details to write about us brothers, sort of *Rumpole* style!" (He was referring to the British TV series about a bumptious barrister and his eccentric male colleagues.)

"Ahh, you might just be right there, Jim!"

Well, if he can speak this way and so affectionately, it's probably okay if I call them The Broze.

Journaling one day, I made a list of the topics that had popped up during the talk over breakfast and multiple pots of coffee: memories of Mom; the Broze' childhood days and the dog next door; Craigville coffee that once tasted like mothballs due to winter storage of grounds next to a Fels Naphtha container; a teacher at Exeter who had seemed "twenty-five feet tall" to Pete, and the controversial English teacher all three suffered through; lens materials for eyeglasses; Obamacare; justices of the Supreme Court; email and spam problems; immigration issues; Lincoln's Civil War generals; and presidential biographies in general.

In Pete's favorite phrase at that time, "There you have it!" A typical Buffington conversation, all over the place, just in a different cottage.

Wherever we were, I kept my camera at the ready, such as the time I found Pete telling stories to the others out in the front yard, gesturing like a conductor and taking up most of the air space. Or in some situation where I could not use the camera, I would remind myself, *Listen carefully, they're at it again! Make sure you remember this so you can get it all down later.*

From across the table in a restaurant booth I would watch the guys elbow each other in the ribs, clink glasses, and compare what they were drinking. Always the Broze leaned back and sipped, cracked jokes, reminisced, and ruminated on the state of the world. Their voices sounded like violas and cellos sawing away, and they were a rumpled bunch with wardrobes running to well-broken-in (make that "tattered") khaki pants or shorts, oxford cloth shirts or faded fraying tees (gotta get your freebie's-worth), and baseball caps. Pete's tee shirts represented the seemingly endless variety of road races he had run over the years.

As well as being age-wise the bookends of the trio, Jim and Andy closely resembled each other: horizontal features, dashes of blue eyes, a line of mouth—and build. Many years back, standing next to Jim on an occasion when Andy was absent, I once caught myself squeezing his hand in a wifely way, so similar was his frame and posture to Andy's. Both men also resembled Mom, Jim almost uncannily at times. He was also the most photogenic, though of course I preferred Andy. Jim often flashed a gleeful, squint-eyed, "Gotcha!" look that I just loved to catch.

As the guys grew older, I noticed a lot of graying hair, jowls, and receding hairlines, plus a characteristic Buffington look: lips very slightly parted, eyes focusing on the distance as their owner revved up to speak. About to launch a bad pun, they all, particularly Andy, would slightly purse their lips; appraising a single malt or a new hot sauce (and in Andy's case, an oyster), you'd get the strong impression of tongue stirrings within.

As for the brother in the middle, in Pete's oval face I could not discern any one forebear. His walrus mustache contributed a broad curve, with thin arches of salt-and-pepper brows above his eyes. Sometimes these gave him a questioning look; they also echoed the curvature of his mostly bald head. Pete was also capable of an occasional smile of great sweetness, mitigating his flood of words; to me it revealed the loving, generous soul beneath a curmudgeonly persona.

Professionally, Pete had lived a long, complex, and colorful life as trust officer at a major New York bank; in retirement he spent his summers at Craigville and the rest of the year enjoyed a wide range of cultural happenings in Manhattan. As oldest, Jim had retired first, from a variety of positions in a life insurance company. Andy never did retire completely; at the cottage he still read and edited physics manuscripts and engaged in long phone calls with colleagues back in California.

Together at Craigville, however, they were still the Broze. The Buffington boys, who sometimes got so verbally wound up that I had to give such prompts as "Your coffee's getting cold!" Or, unable to insert a word, I'd resort to pointing at the coffee pot or their mugs. The Broze also had their own terms for use in driving. Whenever it was hard to get out into traffic from a side road and cars kept coming, Andy or Pete would say, "Close up the gap! They're closing up the gap!" Over and over. Then there was The Impossible Left and the ever-retold story of Pete's accident there when he encountered "Madge from Mashpee." I finally asked for a moratorium on that one.

Madge, though, was one of a select group: the bogeymen, people immortalized in the Broze' pantheon as somehow being In the Way. Of Us. For example, The Dentist. At any mention of tree trimming, "Oh, watch out, if we do anything like that, The Dentist'll be on our backs!" This referred to a member of a local conservation board years before, who snooped around local properties and reported the owners' tree pruning violations. Though probably long since dead, in our cottage he lived. People like him and Madge stood for what stopped us from doing what *we* wanted or should be able to do. Forced to act in observance of local law or regulations, or trying to catch some item on sale, the Broze always assumed the worst. "Oh, we'll *never* be able to get a permit!" Or "They'll be all out of that stuff before we ever get there."

A lurchy bunch, the Broze. I had not exactly selected this society, yet I lived with it. While acting as general provider and stand-in for Mom, and quite good at doing so, I was also the odd man—or woman—out. I got pretty tired of "We're the Buffingtons, we were here first." Or "We know." They did not consciously adopt this stance; I think they could not help it. Also, their verbal brilliance took little or no account of people's feelings and tended to assume its own importance.

So I would take to what I call "bouncing off." I'd leave them to their talk or jobs or expeditions—and pursue my own work.

Is "bouncing off" too mild a term? Was I simply angry at being ignored or stonewalled verbally? Yes, sometimes. But living with Mom had schooled me in turning anger into action, making use of it by learning from it.

Also, I say "bounce" because of the come-back nature of the idea. For I had fun with the guys as well as observing them as a phenomenon, and inadvertently they created a lot of material for me. If I did not waste time on being resentful and left them to verbal sprawl, I made time for my own pursuits. And later I bounced back, refreshed, and we talked or went out to dinner, whatever we had all decided to do. Tour an antique show, gallery, or historical society, or just chat.

Once we simply gathered together on the porch with drinks and enjoyed watching a drenching rainstorm, exchanging whatever thoughts came to mind. I remember Pete's remarking, more than once, "All that water . . . all that water . . . where's it all come from?" And I knew what he meant, and I wondered, too.

Andy's love for his brothers was a good part of why he loved Craigville. I was touched, seeing these men happy together, though one evening, I wrote, "Getting pretty sick of the Broze. I know the phenomenon, it doesn't surprise me, but I want my husband back! Not this loud verbose person so given to exaggeration, as he is with Pete. I know the drill, I signed up for it, and I've had enough for this year."

Yet I would return the next summer. "Andy, Pete and I went out for dinner for Pete's birthday. When we got home, I was ready for some quiet so took a walk in the misty-moisty evening . . . . Came back with misted glasses, frizzy hair. No sharp edges anywhere, the beach all in neutrals, horizon blurred. Seemed appropriate that the dog being walked was a Weimaraner, dark pearly gray, with those moonstone-y eyes that fit right into the prevailing color palette." That walk later figured in an essay I wrote.

Or, "Oh, there is so much to hold, if I could only do it. I am so tired . . . . I wonder, does the stress from human affairs and busyness shove through into consciousness and push out thoughts like my pond thoughts of the afternoon? Would I think as productively if I had all the time I wanted to experience, read, and write? Or is nature here my escape from all these human complications into a world that—even with people around me—I conceive entirely in my own terms?"

I did not always work, or play, alone. I noted, "Andy, Pete, and I have all worked very hard, with common purpose . . . . We are truly making this house a 'kinder, gentler' place. . . . I am feeling melancholy at leaving here in a way I never have before."

"And all around us, the glorious marsh, the bushy, busy trees— busy with squirrels this time of year, acorn gathering. Furry bodies flinging themselves about, flying across air and landing on swaying, dipping oak limbs or chasing up and down trunks. It's so fascinating and fun to watch that I was right with Pete when he said, 'I don't want to trim any branches and limit their activities.'

"Plus all the insects humming at night, the mushrooms and Indian pipe, burgeoning due to dampness . . . cardinals, crows, wrens . . . just the view out the bathroom window. . . . I come here to write . . . ." And be part of the activities, of whatever kind.

BEACH PLUM JELLY

"Here, these are for you!" my nephew Jon said in his growly voice, peering out from under a duckbill hat. Close behind on the path came brother-in-law Jim with his marvelous whole-face grin, holding out a bottle of wine.

Jon handed me a rumpled paper bag full of something lumpy and heavy. I peered in.

"Oh, Jon! Beach plums! Where on earth did you find them?"

Both men laughed and Jon answered, "Right out in my front yard! There's about two pounds in there."

I passed the bag to Andy and Pete, hugged Jon and Jim, and thanked Jim for the wine.

Pete exclaimed, "You mean nobody saw them, people walked right by, and didn't pick 'em? These things are scarce as hen's teeth!" Not only is Jon's house at a major intersection, but one of the roads also leads to a popular beach.

"Nope. They're a bit covered up, I guess, and everybody's in too much of a hurry. Dad and I picked 'em right before we came. They need washing and picking over."

Still flabbergasted at this surprise gift of something so coveted on Cape Cod, so jealously guarded, Pete said, "Hell, of course we'll use 'em! We're gonna make jelly."

I ran to the pantry and came back with an old oblong Limoges serving dish, dumped in the beach plums, and set it on the porch table.

Drinks in hand, we all stood there a moment admiring and then I said, "Oh, I've got to get a picture!"

Complemented by the scalloped edges of the Victorian china with its remnants of gold trim, the plums ranged in color from crimson to cranberry to blueberry, with bits of stem and leaves between. They were not much larger than cultivated blueberries, which some of them resembled. Tiny yellow-orange sockets revealed a spot of inner flesh but not the high proportion of hard round pit within the cloudy marble-sized fruit. Spread out, the plums almost glowed with loveliness and my eyes kept being drawn to them all evening.

A Cape Cod specialty (though they also grow elsewhere on the Atlantic seaboard), beach plums somehow flourish behind sandy bluffs or along the roadside in ground you could not call soil; Thoreau described it as "land . . . no farmer . . . would think of cultivating." Yet these plums make a jelly of magnificent color. Call it cerise, cherry, or crimson, whatever word best conveys clear ruby richness—and their flavor is almost liqueur-like. Most people agree that the fruit must be cooked. Though some say you can eat it raw, no one I know ever has.

Over the years, Mom and Judy gave us jars of beach plum jelly to take back to California. Andy and I always made them last and last. I had never made the jelly myself, and though I had seen it for sale in country-store-type places, I always viewed "the bought stuff" as not quite the genuine article.

However, it was one thing to thank someone who gives you a jar to take home—and quite another to make the jelly. Easy to just talk about it, too. For a few days that was as far as Andy, Pete, and I went.

But we knew the plums would spoil if we didn't get to work, so on the morning of August 24, Andy and Pete took off to buy pectin (Certo) and paraffin (for sealing the jars), although they ended up going several places before they found any. Then, while I cleared the kitchen for action, they reviewed the cache of jelly jars in the cellar. Next, in search of cheesecloth for straining, the three of us took off for a kitchen supply place I had been wanting to explore. When we finally got back, it was lunchtime; I heated up Snow's Clam Chowder as Pete washed the chosen jars. "Got a lotski-wotski of 'em!"

We sat down to chowder, and cheese and crackers. I had managed to dredge up three different jelly recipes, but none of us knew which one Mom used.

"Well, she used pectin, that's why we went and bought it!" Andy said as he blizzarded his chowder with pepper.

"Yeah, we've got to. I've heard that from everyone," I answered. "But I don't understand the proportions. I'm reading the recipe that comes with the Certo, and it's not at all like the one in Mom's *Fanny Farmer* cookbook."

"How many pounds do we have? Oh, and pass the cheese, too," Pete said, comfortable in saggy jeans and a faded, fraying sweatshirt I had long wanted to sneak into the trash.

"Two pounds, Pete. But none of these recipes call for just two pounds of plums."

After much hashing out, we converged on one recipe with Andy's mathematical help, then he took off for the porch with the *New York Times* in hand.

"Okay, you guys are in charge now, I'm sitting this one out!"

Alarmed, Pete said, "Oh, no, you don't!"

I joined in: "We need you!"

Thus dragooned, Andy rounded up pots and utensils, I measured sugar, then Pete and I sorted the plums, laying them out on a paper towel. We discarded only a few.

Andy asked, "Do you know where that thing is that Mom used to use? You know, that perforated conical thing that lets the juices through? And you push and pound the fruit with a wooden mallet?"

"Oh, yeah, I know what you're talking about. Yup, that's what we need." Pete banged pots around in the cupboards, then rummaged in the pantry. "Shit! I can't find it! Damn." More crashing about, then he straightened up and said, "Somebody didn't know what it was, so they probably threw it out. There's too much of that going on around here."

Andy agreed. "It's a shame. The thing's exactly what we need."

Improvising, Andy retrieved a rubber hammer from the cellar and Pete went to work pounding. As the breaking skins went "pluk, pluk" against the colander, Pete said, "It's like you're whacking at ball bearings!"

Now the juice had to simmer for thirty minutes. We took a break, read the paper, and Pete offered us fudge.

Bzzzz! Time now to strain the juice, the life's blood of the jelly. We rigged up a contraption from an old chafing dish frame, inside which was a plastic colander draped with cheesecloth, and underneath, an earthenware casserole dish. A paper towel covered the counter in case of drips. Rube Goldberg would have been proud indeed, though no one disagreed when I said, "I bet Mom had a better system than this!"

Pete lifted the jars out of their sterilizing bath with some old tongs I had never realized were designed for just that purpose. With a steady hand, he poured in the precious juice and Andy sealed each jar with melted paraffin. The discarded plum skins and pits looked like the residue from some ghastly surgery; the jelly resembled liquid rubies.

Eight filled jars sat triumphantly on an old cookie sheet on the counter.

We washed up what seemed like millions of containers and utensils, then I made myself a mug of tea and we all adjourned to the porch and put our feet up. The guys celebrated with a "wee drappie" of Scotch.

During all this, there were several times when I thought, *Oh, dear, now that was a gift horse whose mouth I've looked into thoroughly.* But then, I already knew about culinary gift horses.

Some were wonderful, Carl and Kathy's garden tomatoes, for instance, or bottles of good wine. Other gifts posed challenges, such as the shriveled veggies that someone handed me on arrival, saying, "These look a bit old, but they're still good and I didn't want to leave them while I was away." Then there was the torpedo-like loaf of dark rye whose slices, even toasted, offered all the texture and flavor of a tombstone. Thank goodness for jam.

To me, though, the worst gift horse was fish. Especially at 4 p.m., when it superseded anything you had planned for dinner. Sometimes fish seemed to attain eternal life, like the package of bony little flatties (max six inches in length) that awaited us in the freezer when we arrived one August. Someone's fishing expedition had run into a huge school of scup, a moniker that I think expresses their taste and bony composition—and general worth. After one try, we decided scup was literally "for the birds."

One day when I returned from a trip, I was informed that we had been given bluefish for dinner. Immediately, I remembered a friend of my mother's telling of stealing out in the dark of night to bury blue fish in the garden; her husband had been fishing every day that summer and "The blues were running!" She was greeted with a burst of sympathetic laughter.

Our gift of bluefish turned out to be mercifully small, so I cooked and served them. Then just as I sat down, I had to take a long phone call. When I returned to the table, my plate was cold. I dug in, then thought, *All this tastes like is thick white fish. What's the big deal?*

Pete, who loved the stuff, said, "Oh, bluefish has to be eaten right away to be good."

Ironically, he later described some sole as "a white fish of indeterminate enthusiasm" and right away my inner voice said, *Now that's how I feel about bluefish.*

Still, they were gifts, an aspect of the dance of life with conventions and personal style attached. People brought gifts when they came to stay or for dinner, to be friendly, or to share what they considered special and life-enhancing. Our role was to say "Thank you" and take on the obligation as best we could. Though we could have given the beach plums away, I never considered doing so, nor did Andy or Pete. We just went ahead and made jelly.

The next morning, we tasted it. Pete said, "That's damn good!"

I answered, "It tastes like a lovely wine!" It reminded me of a not-too-dry rosé, clear and fresh. Beach plums are not dark damson-style fruit, so the jelly tasted light, even grapelike, with hints of berries and currants.

Two weeks later, having arrived back in California, I unpacked Andy's and my share. Wrapped in multiple layers of rubber-banded bubble wrap, nestled amongst my underwear, our two jars had crossed the continent in perfect shape.

Holding one in each hand, I remembered our work that day, all that rushing about and fussing. I also remembered Cape Cod. Picked from those sandy dunes or roadsides, beach plums are a reminder of how hardscrabble life on the Cape once was. A "wild, rank place," as Thoreau described it, Cape Cod used to be anything but the pretty vacation area we all love. I was also thankful that beach plum bushes produce more generously than bayberries, another Cape product that grows in dune sand. To make bayberry candles as the Pilgrims did, you need between ten and fifteen pounds of tiny, tiny berries to yield a pound of usable wax. I have never known anyone to take that on.

Later, when I leafed through Mom's diary of fruit picked and jelly made, I also realized what a small batch of plums we had had to work with. In 1980, she recorded, "Peter, Jim [Dad], with a little help from Lois [Mom], picked about 8 quarts beach plums." She went on to note two more batches picked, then the summer's jelly total: "63 glasses [jars] of varied sizes."

Whatever the quantity, making jelly was and is laborious. Will future generations feel it is worth doing? Sharing that glorious red stuff amounted to a kind of communion, which was itself a gift; perhaps the process of making it was another. Perhaps. Or maybe the real gift was the story I can tell, rather than all the work.

Without Mom's preferred recipe, which I came upon a couple of years later, and without a food mill (that tool we could not find), we paid tribute to family tradition as best we could. Only later did I learn that we should also have worked with a mix of ripe and unripe fruit, as the latter contributes natural pectin which helps the jelling process.

Nonetheless, we did it. We created an essence. Pure, clear in color, our beach plum jelly was a compound of all that went into it—and the source of a memorable, complex taste that lingered long after the jars were empty.

THE WOMAN WHO WASN'T THERE

*A*nd what about my counterpart on the family tree, my sister-in-law Judy Buffington? The other creative soul in the family whom I saw whenever I went to Craigville. In my early years, Judy stayed there with her kids for most of the summer.

Back then the Buffingtons held a distinct *en masse* quality for me; also, Judy and Jim lived in Mom's off-season town of East Walpole, Massachusetts, so when I visited, she and Mom seemed to have a modus operandi all worked out, cordial or not.

Seeing Judy, however, did not mean she and I spent much time together. Among the family or distracted by our kids, some of our encounters were little more than sightings. Judy buzzed about like a human Roomba, seldom lingering for more than a moment or two. When we did talk at any length, Judy was fascinating: a bristling, buzzing personality in a small package (she was not much over five feet tall); the term *rough diamond* comes to mind.

Over the years I knew her, Judy's creativity was clear, whether she expressed herself in painting (watercolor or tempera), decorative designs on objects, crewel embroidery, cooking, or stained glass. She often gave us gifts she had made or decorated.

As for coming to see us in California, after just one visit Judy traveled only to other places. Andy and I felt we were granted snippets of relationship, though each encounter was intense, sometimes warm and friendly, as were her letters. Over time, though, Judy grew opinionated and frequently sharp, sometimes prickly; ease, let alone intimacy, was a sometime thing with her. Her sons' struggles with alcohol and drugs caused her great anguish and shadowed her other relationships. However, she loved my daughters and loyally kept in touch with them. And her death from leukemia in 2008 at age seventy-four hit us all hard, especially as I so often thought how alive Judy was.

I still think of her as part of Craigville, rather as though she were arresting, distant glass I keep looking at for its intense color. Judy was a fellow artist, and my friend.

Oh, her stained glass! In the last five or so years of her life, Judy's creative spirit blossomed; she went far beyond her early small-scale painting and needlework. I think, too, that she was as freed by Mom's death as I was—maybe even more so, as she and Jim lived nearest to Mom and loyally assisted her to the end.

In her glass, Judy colored outside the lines, so to speak, refusing to be restricted to conventional frames and shapes. She incorporated bases and bowls from broken dishes as well as slices of geodes. Sometimes the outer edges of her pieces sort of bulged; supposedly round edges came out sharp and craggy; in the intensity of designing and making, she must have forgotten everything else and pushed forward exactly as she wanted. Although she worked early on from kits or patterns like the oval heron medallion at Craigville, her heart was not in them. For instance, she could not resist implanting yet more of those jewel-like cabochons. Sometimes this practice over-stuffed a design and created rounds that were slightly out of true.

I loved her sea mandalas. Roughly circular medallions about sixteen inches in diameter, they look as though she had brought the beach home, having somehow gathered up a wave's worth of shells and ripples. Entirely her own forms and layouts, each one is visual music, complete and rich and free and varied. Each one is alive.

I am privileged to own one she made for me, though it is slightly smaller. Its primary design element is a large, veined scallop shell in tiny-bubbled glass the color of morning mist, surrounded by curving natural shapes in sapphire and milky blue, also one vaguely whale-shaped piece in soft gray-green. Like pebbles carried by the sea, cherry-sized discs of aqua and clear glass range in and around among the pieces.

When I thanked her, Judy was gracious but confessed that the piece was not her best work. Though she knew that I regard the scallop shell as beautiful and as a personal symbol, she confided that she had not inhabited this piece creatively. The scallop had gotten in her way. Though touched by her kindness, I could sense her unease. Judy had to be herself only. Yet she had created something especially for me. I treasure her reaching out even as I feel, yes, the piece is somewhat flawed—and as a reminder to be honest myself, to be sure that what I put out in public is true to what I think or value.

Judy also created many oblong glass mosaics that created privacy while admitting light. Among the many vertical opaque or textured bar-shaped component pieces, there are usually one or two clear ones somewhere, safe spots from which to look out onto the world, but not be seen oneself. At first, I felt these "screens" were rather safe artistically; but as I have lived with them, noticing the views through them in changing light, they have come to seem more complex and fascinating, even cagey.

Though she studied glasswork with a fine local craftsman, Judy's impatience often ran away with her, especially in regard to cutting the glass itself and with learning to solder and handle leading.

Yet I applaud her stubborn inventiveness even as I note imperfections, especially one eighteen-inch-diameter mandala with a winning color scheme of clear glass and royal blue. Surrounded by a brilliant pointy starburst, its blue center is a deep blue breast-like shape, pointed and jutting out like a torpedo perhaps three or four inches. (Its original use was as the bowl of a footed dessert dish.) Only if you view it from alongside do you fully "get the point" and wonder, *Did she really want that effect?*

I am sure she did. Judy was herself. Unashamedly.

Inwardly sure or not, Judy was fierce—and always wanted to appear so. To whom? I think herself first, then the rest of us. Padding about her house, Judy was a compact bundle of intensity who knew just how she wanted things. She did not want to be helped. We all knew the refrain: "I'll do that, Sally, you sit down!"

Her writing was one of the most dominant hands I have ever seen: an elegant right-slanting script with closely spaced letters that stacked together and looked like leaning tiles. Close to vertical, it gave the impression of multiple arguments or reasons lined up to support her point of view. Her script practically bristled, and you knew who had written the instant you saw it.

Outspoken? Of course. Also, of all the Buffingtons, Judy was the only one who ever asked what the rest must also have wondered: "Are you ever coming back East to live, Sally?"

This came at me out of the blue one evening, as we were returning from watching the sunset at First Encounter Beach. I can see us: two women walking along the gray ribbon of road in Eastham, faces turned toward each other, with the yellow-green of salt marsh reeds behind us. Judy in her characteristic white blouse, blue denim skirt, and Keds, I in shorts and a bright top.

"No, Judy, I think I'm a Californian now. I still love it here, and I'll never stop coming east in the summer, but we've made our lives out there and we're happy. Besides, there's Andy's job, and you know he can't just up and move; jobs are scarce in his field."

A silence fell. That was the last I heard of it.

If we had moved back East, perhaps Judy and I would have managed to share more music, for we both loved it deeply. Judy was not only a lifelong opera afficionado but also a superfan of the American soprano Eleanor Steber; at one point Judy compiled a handsome collection of tributes to Steber, *He Loves Me When I Sing*. She spent much time soliciting these tributes, then collating, designing, and privately publishing the book.

Some family members, though, considered her book extravagant, also unnecessary. I felt that all her labor and creativity were in service of someone else's art and wished that instead, Judy would step forth as an artist herself. I did not, however, have the guts to tell her. Later, when the printed edition did not sell out, we had to keep Judy from destroying the remaining several hundred copies. I was horrified at the way she took against it, how vehement she was.

Yet after Judy died, a friend of hers told me, "Judy was always the type that slammed the door when something didn't work out."

Does canceled-out opportunity (no matter who does the canceling) explain why Judy steamed through her days? Why she kept busy, busy, busy, and often seemed to leave little or no room for leisure or thinking? At times she seemed to me to cut off her own creativity, and to act in ways that appeared as a kind of personal penance. Except for stained glass.

I have never been one to destroy finished work. Schooled by years of practicing music, I keep slogging away. As for writing, I keep thinking and revising, also often trying to figure how or where a failed piece of work might improve or serve some other need.

When I first began to write, I felt close enough to Judy that I shared my poems with her; she was warm in her praise and told me she kept a special drawer for what I sent. However, perhaps my prose (or its subjects and boldness) became too much for her, as I witnessed one summer evening in 2006.

I had arrived at Craigville feeling terribly down, having come from a writing workshop where my essay received a storm of criticism. When Judy invited us over for a family dinner a couple of days later, I thought, *Oh, how nice! That'll be a great change. I'd love to see her and Jim, and be in their lovely house, and it'll be fun to see their boys, too.*

As always, Judy served a delicious meal. Afterward, seated at one end of the table, I got into a long conversation with her and son Jon, who is an artist. Judy asked about the workshop, so I briefly recounted my painful experience. Then we got to discussing how to give criticism. Mostly listening, Jon seemed surprised at the flood of talk between his mother and me.

"I don't mind taking criticism and I'm used to it, Judy—and I know I'll get over this. But I don't see any need to demoralize the student in the process."

"Oh, Sally, you're just too nice! And you expect other people to be! How else will you learn?" Judy fired back.

"I think there's all sorts of ways to learn. Also, I've been a teacher myself for a long time and I know how to lead people into learning without destroying their confidence. I've done it many times." *Drat, these chairs are hard, I wish I had a cushion.*

"You just coddle them!"

"No, I don't think so. And this workshop should have been better led. If someone's in charge, I trust him or her to keep the group's feedback from turning into a group attack. Besides, it gives the impression that your work is altogether bad, when probably that's not true." Jon was listening intently, his face turning from Judy to me and back.

Judy took another sip of her drink. "Well, maybe your piece just wasn't good enough!" She spoke loudly and had gotten red in the face.

"I thought it was pretty strong before I went, but I realize that I need to learn how much musical detail people can understand or want to know." (I was then writing a memoir about my flute-playing career.) *I'm going to back off. This is getting too heated, and I'm not going to mess up the occasion . . . . Damn, I'm so tired. And now I'm getting discouraged all over again.*

Judy bore down on me, her voice getting harsh. "You've got to work harder, Sally, and get a thicker skin! And besides, what you said about the *Voice of Firestone* soprano in the essay you showed me just wasn't <u>true</u> . . . . You're wrong about that!"

What detail? I had not maligned her favorite Eleanor Steber, but I had described another soprano as having a "fruity" voice. Had I demeaned another idol? Or gotten too big for my britches? Perhaps Judy found me too much. Had I trod on her territory with my reference to any soprano? Or maybe she had had too many drinks.

After that evening, I kept my writing pretty much private, though of course I did not stop. I also continued to attend critique groups and workshops.

I have since wondered if Judy's seemingly strong ego had a brittle side. Brisk and dominant though she appeared, was there a frightened or worried child within her? Or someone who never got her way to the extent she wanted?

And how about Craigville? We both knew that territory. Judy had had to co-exist with Mom there many summers before I came along. Forceful, organized, and energetic, both of them were bright women who operated with a strong sense of home and family—and of being the domestic boss. Share the cottage? Oh, dear. I have heard about their epic battles. Searching for a metaphor in that contest of wills, I might well supply "broken glass."

A story from before my time. Judy had gone out for the evening and returned late, only to find that she did not have her key. Loath to knock and wake people, dreading explanations, she broke a window to get a hand in and twisted open the front doorknob. Damage done, she got in and went to bed.

Not just any window—Judy broke the Victorian beveled-glass front door panel. Someone said, "Couldn't you have chosen some plain glass instead of that one? Or gotten in some other way?"

Instantly criticized, Judy was branded "impulsive," a label that has stuck ever since. Soon a replacement pane of plain glass was put in place and for years that was what I thought belonged there. The deed has never been forgotten and it seems to me that Judy was never forgiven, either. No other window would have been any better; she would have incurred blame no matter what. And the door was only property. Yet it was also the front door—with antique glass—to the summer sanctuary of a property-conscious family.

Many years later at Andy's suggestion, Judy designed and made a replacement panel. In the style of the original, it is a pleasing composition of pointed vertical lozenges, rectangles, and triangles of plain, stippled, and ripple-patterns, in shades of blue and green and clear glass.

One more story, which Judy herself shared with me in a letter. Again, the story is from before my time, but it illuminates her and my struggles with Mom.

After some argument, Mom told her, "Dad and I didn't bring you up, so you don't know how to act, and that's why we can't forgive you!"

While I am surprised (and skeptical) that Mom ever said this, the substance is right on. The essence of the in-law relationship: you can never be one of *us,* you will never achieve—perhaps not even come close to—the way *we* do things.

I need to remember also that Judy and I were in-laws to each other. In our early meetings, I know she liked me very much and she must have hoped I would move back East and live closer, both as a friend and as a buffer in dealing with Mom. However, distance forever shadowed Judy and my relationship, too.

I doubt that Judy considered herself anyone who would teach me or supply me with an example of a creative person. She was who she was, and damn the torpedoes. In her early years, she had cherished dreams of becoming an operatic soprano and getting the kind of conservatory training I had; how realistic those hopes were, I do not know, especially as singing voices operate by different rules than instrumental playing, with which I am familiar.

Far from writing of "someone who wasn't there," I am writing of a complex, elusive woman whose personality was as multifaceted (and sometimes as sharp-edged) as the glass she worked with, and full of different lights, different angles.

Trying to capture Judy, I need all these metaphors, and then some. Forceful, energetic, emotional, she was like a colorful, high-speed wind that occasionally whistled through my life.

Or I think of her like a flavoring: Extract of Judy. Whether a drop or half teaspoonful or single visit, it always had to last me a long time.

I have always wished for more.

Sometimes I wishfully think of Judy as a kind of creative sister in the cottage, an ally; yet she was both "a sometime thing" (to use Ira Gershwin's words) and more of a challenge than I bargained for. Often,

I view her as a muse seen through those glass pieces I enjoy living with and admire. They are easier to live with than Judy in person.

Judy died too soon, with so much more she wanted to create. I hear her voice within me now, whispering insistently: *Keep working, keep creating, don't let anything stop you. You have been given the time, Sally—use it.*

OPENING

*H*elp Wanted: Cook/kitchen/accommodations manager for great old summer cottage, to provide meals for vocal family. Must be flexible individual. Carrying meals to screen porch required. Good listener desired. Workspace: Old-fashioned kitchen with little counter space. Duties: Deal with marketing and specialty purveyors, some hold family warrant (Four Seas Ice Cream). Benefits: interesting people, charming though funky accommodations, short walk to beach, and use of antique serving dishes.

I wrote this job description for fun, yet it expressed something significant about the situation I found myself in at Craigville after Mom died, one probably familiar to many other daughters-in-law. A vital cog in the family wheel, now I was the Mrs. Buffington everyone depended upon, the CDO—Chief Domestic Officer, if you will.

Yet I had no vote in major cottage matters, such as decisions on insurance or possible land conservation donation. Though I could and did express opinions and I worked hard, my status amounted to second-class citizenship. I was not one of the owners' circle.

Oh, I could do a bunch of fun, lady-of-the-house things like buying flowers and bright new table linens; I could get rid of all those white towels I had hated for years and buy more practical dark-colored ones. I lightened up menus, too, and we began eating dinners out on the porch and loving it. And wherever we ate, I made sure that no longer would people be served too much or something they did not like—and no longer would anyone be rousted out of bed for breakfast.

More importantly, I tried to avoid handing down edicts or making pronouncements; I also tried to keep hurts or misunderstandings from festering. I worked at listening to people and did what I could to help the whole place run with a "live and let live" point of view.

But in some critical matters, I came up against a wall known as a nominee trust, a legal strategy that had been set in place with the purpose of avoiding estate taxes when Mom died; this had named the three Buffington sons, Jim, Pete, and Andy, as owners/trustees. (During her lifetime, Mom had been so dominant that I seldom thought much about the trust or what it might feel like not to be an owner myself.)

In one sense, however, I had lived in this position before; during my teen years, I could not have legally held ownership status in my parents' cottage rental business. Yet I always felt like an owner: my opinion mattered and I felt that I had much to do with whether we succeeded. My parents shared their purposes and thoughts with me; they also relied on me for a good deal of work: lawn mowing, cottage cleaning, answering the phone, showing cottages for rental, delivering linens, and making beds. Emotionally I was *in*, though I knew little or nothing of their anxious dealings with the local bank.

Even on my epochal first winter visit to Craigville back in 1968, I had figured that since I was to marry a Buffington son, someday he and I would come into ownership of the cottage, though partially. While I was in no rush, sooner or later, this would happen.

Now my thoughts surfaced as a fitful series of questions, often blurted out by me to me, or drifting through my mind. What did owning Craigville mean? And this in-law business, how about that? Was this place worth the struggles I sometimes went through, and what could I learn or gain from it all?

Expressing a different opinion from Andy or Pete, or making no headway when I suggested a change, I was sometimes met by the old phrase Andy had used with our kids: "Just manage." Invoked when somebody wanted something and one or the other parent (or both) thought the need could wait, the phrase meant "Just get along, come up with other ideas, or find a different solution."

At Craigville, I did all of these.

Could I have been named a trustee or an owner? I never asked. That is the basic question, though. And would things have come out differently?

Yes, the trust could have been changed. But I would have had to fight hard, even bitterly—and I would surely have lost loving relationships. By nature, I am someone who wants to get along and is uncomfortable at being in major disagreement. Over time, I weighed the pros and cons and decided that challenging the long-held "blood relatives only" position would not be worth the struggle. However quirky or irritating they might be, I had come to know and love my Buffington relatives and I had no stomach for a fight.

I suppose you could say I settled. That is, I gave in on this major point, one that others might consider something due me. The irony is that their cottage seemed to give itself to me; also, the place was and is so wonderful. Nobody could take that away from me, nor all the experiences, memories, sensations, and, yes, essays, and this book.

Eventually I came to feel that I perhaps owned Craigville more than any of them, due to my work and in-depth residence, as well as long, sustained thinking. Interloper though I might be, I was a knower and possessor.

Thus I thought of things most family members probably did not indulge in, including a fantasy of being alone in the cottage. In all these years, I spent one night there solo. I remember enjoying myself, albeit with a distinct sense of unreality, for the family custom has always been that we are always at the cottage *together*. "We" means any and all Buffingtons who are available at the time you want to go.

To have the whole house to myself: now that would be the ultimate in selfish pleasure. I could wander at length wherever I pleased. I could dig into drawers and closets, read other people's letters, even! Get nosey. I might sit among dust motes and shadows, wander among all the old furniture and curios, or, mole-like, burrow down under in the basement. There I would pick up a couple of Andy's jars of screws and fasteners and shake them for clinks and jingles, trying to conjure up all the incidents that had gone on and coax out ghostly voices still lurking among the cobwebs in the corners. Back upstairs, I might morph into a spirit and join all the other ghosts floating about near the ceilings . . . or snoop under beds, especially Pete's, to see what treasures he had stashed there. As though I were the only person who mattered here, a creative soul wandering her territory . . . . How much more possessive could I get? To creep or walk or skulk, or stride about in a kind of trance . . . to sink into every corner and drawer, every nook and cranny . . .

Or just sit in perfect quiet and be.

Another clue to my role was a public moment remembered from my daughter's wedding. The next morning, I had served Sunday brunch on the porch; and afterwards, we said goodbye to the groom's parents and brothers. About to leave for Nova Scotia, our new counterparts now stood along the path outside the front porch. Andy, Pete, Anne, and I learned over the railing.

Smiling broadly, David's dad, Fred, said, "Well, we're very proud that Katherine's a member of *our* family, too—she's a Swain now!" They all beamed and everyone laughed.

My face must have fallen. Even though what he said was perfectly true, I was not ready for it. However, before I could reply, Fred added, "But she's only 49% ours. She'll always be 51% yours, a Buffington!" Quick pick-up! He had correctly read my dismay.

Although Fred sounded a bit numerical for the emotional reality, the numbers speak of something. I have come to think that a one percent of intrinsic family-ness exists on each side of a marriage, which put together constitutes an in-law zone, a buffer between total belonging to either one. A real but invisible barrier. That two percent stands for a place in the middle, perhaps a line, even—and sometimes it swells to larger size.

Perhaps my desire to be an actual owner of Craigville was an attempt to cross that line—which I could never do legally. But with time, I would find my own ways around it, and perhaps transform the zone for my own purposes.

One of my primary ways sprang from my journals, which soon took on the dual role of private cottage yearbooks and logbooks. Based on this data, I began to write essays to understand what I had been through with Mom, or prose poems about cooking, swimming, Cape Cod itself, or discoveries made when I walked. Some of those writings were rambling first attempts that my writing group kindly suffered through; some are part of this book. With time to think and write, often while Andy and Pete undertook repair jobs around the house, I began to study the cottage and what a treasure I had, even partially, come into.

As far as I could see, Craigville was already mine in ways the rest of the family didn't engage in; it would become more so if I felt and noticed and kept alert to all its fascinations. Perhaps direct confrontation over business decisions was something I could leave to others—I had found a muse.

Still, was I settling for something less than I wanted or should have wanted? Or was I just being realistic about a situation I could not change without causing a family earthquake?

Even though Craigville was not the adventurous refuge in nature I had dreamed of as a teenager, and not Andy's and mine to design as we pleased, it was a place we were an integral part of, and on Cape Cod, our toehold. Though I would dream about beautiful properties I saw advertised in the *Cape Codder*, I never considered buying one. Not only would such a thing complicate life for Andy and me, but the cottage at Craigville kept revealing itself further, giving me a place to find myself.

A journal entry: "10:20, I'm the last one standing, Pete and Andy are in bed.

"In our front yard, picking out the not-quite-round moon from among branches. I walk to the edge of the foliage and look first out over the marsh, then turn 180 degrees back toward the house. Our house, our beloved old ark, its main outline just discernable among the dark and trees, living room and dining room windows bright with light. Our big old box of a house, our family box, it is.

"And somehow I feel lonely—and oddly comfortable in solitude— and between two worlds here. I do love the place, and I am ready to go home. As a writer, I don't fit very well here. I do know who I am, but I wonder over and over whether they want much to know me or what I think or write, who I am. And I sort of—only sort of—belong to/in one of these old family boxes around us in this village, yet I live here for a while each summer . . . . The great lighted houses, anchored arks, and I am alone, in and around one of them. I am in the light, amid the salty, windy dark—alone within them all."

I also began to realize what I had come into: an odd funky old place and its surroundings. I wrote, "I will never not be of this place." The cottage offered a pan-sensory existence. Every time we arrived, my pores would open. On meeting the fusty, musty air, I'd throw open the windows! I experienced the cottage through my feet on the stairs, my hands on paring knives or ripening fruit, my fingers on a pen rushing over the pages of my notebook or stacking plates in the dishwasher. My nose sensing something burning on the stove or my ears picking up the sizzle of a boil-over, and my cook's sensitivity knowing when brownies were ready to take out of the oven. My hands and arms at work, lifting furniture or folding laundry or hanging it out on the clothesline. My ears recognizing bird calls or footsteps on the path or the clink of ice cubes in a glass. My feet reveling in the springiness of dry leaves out in the woods.

The house was marking me, taking me in. And even as I felt a certain displacement, I was creating ownership on my own terms, seizing on that strange two percent of in-law-ship and expanding it into my thinking. Slowly it grew into something that no one else had:

an eventual self-created, self-granted deed to Craigville, and my license to discover and find myself there. I would have and hold.

But all this would take time, and it would happen gradually, in fits and starts.

BOUQUET

*H*ere is what I gathered on my walk this morning: four Queen Anne's lace, detailed white blooms composed of dozens of little starbursts on plain green stems, and two dry gray branches of bayberry that appear almost ancient yet are somehow beautiful. They occupy a clear, footed vase about ten inches high shaped like an old soda fountain glass. Lying on the table before them is a gray seagull feather with a black tip.

About nine o'clock, I start off through Craigville to the bluff, then take The Forty Steps down to the channel-like path between fence and tangled woods. I head toward the beach, and when I get there the place seems so clean and simple that it resembles a young child's drawing: tan sand, dark blue water, and sky-blue sky. Like a child, I cannot resist picking up a feather to bring home.

Eventually I take Long Beach Road (yes, there is also a Short Beach Road), lined with Martha-Stewart–type residences complete with gardens, gardeners, and people to mow the beautiful lawns. Behind on the left is the shore; behind houses on the right, the Centerville River. Most of the river homes are tricked out with private docks and boats, but all come with a peaty marsh smell. Prim and formal places, except for one with a *buzz!* Bees love its border garden full of ageratum, alyssum, and impatiens. I am sorry when the sound abruptly ends at the driveway.

Having turned around, now the sun is in my eyes as I take the land side of the main beach road. Getting hot! I pass weather-beaten rental cottages with scrub grass lawns and paint flaking around the window frames. Two snack bars, then a trim motel with sunglassed guests stretched out on chaises on the deck: leisure in progress. Not so next door, though. "SunniSands Motel" is in foreclosure, bleakly transformed by a winter of boarded-up windows and doors. Sheets of cloudy plastic flap forlornly around its sign, shredded by the wind.

I turn onto the marsh road now, fine, soft sand furrowed with jeep tracks. Even the sparse shade of a few scrub pines creates a pleasant drop in temperature. Overhead a goose soars, honking lustily. Then I take the marsh path, past where the river turns and starts its meander up toward the reed field we see from our porch, an extended low thicket with little open water.

Along the path, down to my right, I spot a big patch of Queen Anne's lace and yield to the temptation to pick. Just a few! Straightening up, my eyes meet pine trees with needle-jammed branches and young green cones almost splitting open, they are so full of life. Looking down once more, I find bayberry and break off a couple of twigs, Puritan-austere and pewter colored. Behind them, a bank of cedars presents dense branches studded with light blue berries the size of peas.

Thoroughly hot and sticky now, eager for leafy shade, I tramp up a small rise into Craigville. *Eau de garbage.* A truck has just collected from the dumpster behind the conference center. What a mix of smells! Is this "bouquet" the nasal equivalent of oil swirls on water? Turning, I walk past an amazing garden: crayon-hued tuberous begonias, colorful plate-sized dahlias, and spreads of cerise and white impatiens.

Home. I tramp up our path, grab the key from its ledge over the porch, twist it in the lock, and kick open the sticky old door. Start some coffee! I put my fistful of bayberry and Queen Anne's lace in water, carry it and the feather out to the porch, and flop down. I am hot all over but my face feels especially flushed, so it feels good to sit and watch a blue jay amongst the leaves. I follow its flight to the rim of the bird bath. A squirrel leaps out of a tree, carrying a large nut, and disappears under dry brown leaves where I hear and see its commotion. Nutless, it reappears and scampers back up the trunk.

On the table, Queen Anne's lace bobs slightly in the invisible tubes of breeze filtering through the screen. For all their detail, these flowers are sparely put together: stem, lace doily stuck on the end. It is as though the plant had decided to concentrate on just that one operation. By contrast, the bayberries cluster in small groups all along their stem; their leaves burst out right at the end like bunched fingers. Neat and self-contained, the gull feather is yet another essay in creation. All its vanes fall in perfectly graduated parallels. The softest of grays, it features an eyebrow of white and a satiny black tip.

Just a few things from along the path. Somehow, though, my bouquet seems finer and richer than anything in the gardens I saw: what the land would produce if left to itself. Yet people live and work and vacation here, and their presence also creates a kind of mixed bouquet. As do all the impressions I gathered on my walk, my response to beach and marsh, this morning in August.

I open my journal, pull the cap off my pen, and start to write.

And there was the word. "Home." And I had made myself even further at home by settling down on the porch to write. That place so treasured by us all in the family, a jointly owned place in a family house. And here I was solo, walking in and acting as if I owned it.

ONE OLD CHAIR

"*H*ave a seat!"

Coming out on the porch, chances are good you will choose or be offered the old white chair. It's handy. Quirky, homely, yet somehow charming, people notice it: the thing has character. Wooden, with a rounded back and woven cane seat, it was probably made around the turn of the twentieth century. To pick up or pull it toward you, put your middle three fingers into an opening in the back shaped like a mustache; the opening is much the same shape as the back piece itself. Condition-wise, the paint's getting thin and the chair is battle-scarred where people have twined their feet around the legs or bumped into something while hauling it around.

Sitting down, you find that the curved arms and vertical spindles support you: sit up and speak your mind! Though not that popular Cape Cod style, a captain's chair, this seat takes no nonsense from anybody, at least no more so than normal

Buffington puffery and freewheeling talk. It is not the best choice for eating dinner, though—I always opt for something more relaxingly angled, also less snug on the hips.

The old white chair. It is the only one like it in the house. It is one of us. To me, if any single piece of furniture could be said to embody the Buffington family, this is it.

And now I had taken charge of that chair. No—taken possession of it, on my own terms. And to me, new terms.

One August afternoon, sun animated the chair's shadow and created such a long sidewise outline on the screen porch's green Astroturf, I half expected one of Edward Gorey's languid heroines to waft by and collapse into it with an elegant little wail.

I grabbed my camera. I had to catch the way the soft gray-black shadow looked as though it had been drawn with a pencil, with spindles almost like tree branches. Transformed into something like a Boston rocker, the entire chair had stretched way out and its cane seat had become a woven light screen. Only a tiny part of the real thing showed: the white tips of three wooden feet tethered this floating spirit-chair.

Then the light shifted, or perhaps a cloud moved across the sun.

The chair sat back up, its normal white self once again. Gorey's lady had wafted off into the woods. A solid citizen once more, I could almost hear the chair snorting and harrumphing. "None of this airy-fairy stuff for me!"

The chair had existed for decades before I came along and took the photo, and perhaps its longevity and stature are appropriate to the status I now accord these images. Going further, the "shadow chair" image might well be the most important one of my whole photographic and creative life. August 16, 2009.

For the sentence above, "I grabbed my camera," should be accompanied by a cymbal crash. *Shazam!* I had begun to really use a camera. To capture the world for myself. In the same way word processing had given me the instrument with which to write, the digital camera had set me free.

Always before, I had felt awkward about taking photographs, even cowed. At the cottage, Andy and Mom each had Leicas and often discussed both their cameras and photos at length. Like most kids, I had begun with a Brownie; later I enjoyed an Instamatic, but except for a brief foray with a Yashica and one exposure to darkroom work way back, photography was something I knew only from an audience standpoint. I had long loved historic and museum-level work; I had studied many exhibits and books on art photography.

But I had never felt natural or at ease taking photographs. For one thing, you had to buy film and wait for it to be developed—and not waste any. Film was precious, also expensive. In addition, I had little technical know-how and was put off by jargon and specs. Serious or even moderately successful photography seemed beyond me, plus of course I was already busy, in a technical sense, playing the flute and later, writing.

Yet it had always seemed to me that if you had taken a picture, you *knew* something. You had command of the situation or the memory.

Finally, in 2008, I bought my first digital camera, a high-level point-and-shoot affair. At Craigville, I began to keep it on the table by the front door, ready to grab on a moment's notice. Whenever I went somewhere, I would toss the camera in my handbag or pocket.

Oh, it was wonderful! Not only was my reach into the world extended, but the zoom stretched my eyes' reach even farther. I could follow a bird's flight to its perch on a telephone pole or read a faraway sign; conversely, I might zero in on moss or a feather or crackled paint on an antique canvas in a museum. And all this in a neat, small package nestled in the palm of my hand.

Even better, I could see what I had just taken; I could judge images in the court of my own mind. Mistakes were an instant erase away. And what were mistakes anyway? Revisions or experiments I could just make and forget if I wished. I could review a day's images and try again the next day. I became photo-greedy, taking multiple images, circling my subject and recomposing, daring myself to try this or that, and defying some of the strictures I had been given as a child, particularly the old "Don't shoot into the sun." I took whatever I wanted, when and where I wanted; if something did not work, I deleted, then tried something else. Another angle, another slant on the idea. Sometimes I even found wisdom in old advice.

I was playing a new instrument.

Being at Craigville—being anywhere—would never be the same again.

But capturing that brief moment of sun, chair, and shadow was significant in yet another way. A couple of days after the shadow chair image, I got a call from California, from the board of nominations at my church: would I take the job of Moderator?

For years I had always responded when the church asked. Acting on faith was, and is, deeply important to me. In this case, I was of course pleased that the committee felt I was capable of the job—but knew what I would be getting into. As the church's chief lay officer, I would preside over many meetings (and sit through them), receive thousands of phone calls and emails and other interruptions, and take on major responsibility. All this for the next two years. I thanked the committee member who had called and asked for time to think. Then I started pondering and praying.

That evening at the desk, I was going over the day's images. Which were worth keeping? What to erase, what could I improve? I came to the shadow chair and found myself smiling. The thought sprang to mind: *I see things other people don't see.*

Over and over, I switched back and forth between fantasy chair and real chair. *Shadow chair. . . plain old white chair . . . . Which one? . . . I need both . . . . My thinking needs to stretch and grow like the lines of that shadow—I have got to keep time open to write and photograph. I must honor my own work, let my creativity flow.*

The next day, I called back and said no.

In that thought process, as has often happened, I had put into words something whose full significance I did not yet understand.

"Keep time open to write and photograph . . . ." Writing and photography: I did both these things. I was to live into understanding how closely they intertwined, and only much later realize how deeply the two would become integrated within me.

Yet, as many as five or ten years before that moment, people had already commented on my writing, "I can just see what you're writing about, Sally, you're so visual." Now that I could see better, I would become more myself.

Also, I did not then realize how I would come to use my photographic archives of Craigville. I would come to mine a photo not only for accuracy in detail, but also the mood of a time or my own depth of involvement, or the changes in people over the summers, or inspiration when I got stuck describing a place or time. Often, too, whenever I began a day's writing, I would set in place a keynote image, something that captured the subject I was writing about or offered a sense of "Oh, you're back, Sally! Come on in."

Words and photographs, verbal and non-verbal input; now I was complete. I had my creative equipment at hand.

A chair is only a possession, a piece of worldly goods. I know that the Bible says, "Lay not up for yourselves treasures on earth . . ." (Matthew 6:19). But seeing the old white chair that way was a sign that reached in and imprinted itself on my spirit.

That chair? That banged-up old white chair on the porch, which everyone used, that had been around for years? Yup. I had seen its possibilities. No one else had ever taken a photograph of it, let alone imagined fanciful connections and visions.

So what else might also offer itself here? The family and its stories, the antiques and charming foreign souvenirs, the framed pictures we all loved, the views, the curiosities—so much was lurking in this place! *Just think, Sally, this whole cottage is full of inspiration. Keep looking around. Look, look harder than anyone else. Write, photograph all you want! You are going to find wonderful things and ideas. Do it. Look for what other people do not see or notice.*　•

AWAKE IN THE NIGHT

A humid August night. 3 a.m. Hardly a sound indoors or out. The leaves hung limp, the birds and usual humming insects were enervated into silence. Every bed in the cottage was occupied.

Andy and I always sleep in the buff; that night I could not have imagined anything else. Each of us lay in a flung position; he was zonked out, but my mind was rushing around counting people, bedroom by bedroom. *What shall we have for breakfast? Have we got enough eggs on hand? Who's leaving? Who arrives today? What on earth can I serve for dinner that everyone will like—and can eat?* Then I drifted toward happier thoughts: how the water had felt this afternoon, and that glorious drive on Route 6A where the trees met above the road in an endless canopy of green, a swaying fabric of leafiness.

I have to write.

Silently I got up, not bothering to put on a robe. I needed no flashlight either and started down the stairs to the living room. The stillness was thick and lovely, the air almost furry on my skin. I had gotten about halfway when I heard a voice.

"Sally?"

Peering around, I made out our friend Howard sitting on the porch in his pajamas, probably desperate for a smidge of breeze. Startled, I froze and reflexively crossed my arms in an X over my breasts.

"Howard, are you okay? Do you need anything?"

"Oh, I'm all right. I just couldn't sleep and it's a bit cooler out here."

"Well, if you want a cold drink, help yourself to what's in the fridge. The light's on a string overhead right as you walk into the kitchen." Then, hoping he had seen no more of me than legs and feet, I turned and scampered back upstairs.

I think back on that night now with only mild embarrassment. Howard probably thought, "Oh, here's someone else who's awake!" (Ever since then, I have always put on a robe when I get up in the night.) I envision myself as I must have looked, my naked figure white among dark shadows: a buxom ghost. In that moment I see myself as the cottage's resident spirit or perhaps Barrie's Peter Pan looking for his shadow when everyone is asleep.

My shadow? Whatever spiral-bound book I was using for a journal that summer. I kept it on the desk or, if my guest-bedroom office were being slept in (it was), in an unused corner of the living room. I sensed my journal waiting for me, glowing in the dark, a rectangle whose luminescence only I could see. To write, however, I would have had to switch on a light, then sit down to write. Probably in the bathroom, the way I had written in motel rooms over the years. Step one, write a word or two, step forward, another word or phrase—and my pen would stride off over the smooth ground of the paper.

Many times over our summers at Craigville, I used the phrase "awake in the night" to begin such journal entries. I was the noticer who recorded what moved her, while others slept or simply lived. No matter when I wrote, I felt myself in a kind of night where I could enter and live in a "myself when naked" attention to the world, with no barriers.

However, I also wrote with others present, perhaps much as Jane Austen operated at Chawton in Hertfordshire, where I saw her writing table in the dining room. She drafted all of *Pride and Prejudice* on a prim surface scarcely large enough for a teacup. Apparently, Austen often scooted in from kitchen or garden to note down ideas. She must have been skilled at using sudden pockets of time and probably she, like me, was stimulated by family activity and those famous "turns about the room."

For instance, an August day at Craigville I recorded when dear friends were visiting. "Outside, glistening oak leaves and the sounds of large drops plopping from the gutter pipe. A *lovely* day to be indoors! Carl and Andy are playing Bach, and Pete's on the porch with the paper, coffee, and radio for company. Kathy's holed up on the couch with a book. The house is a clutter of sheet music, dropped clothes, books, and magazines, Carl's oboe case, used coffee mugs, newspapers—all accompanied by the constant watery percussion of rain." I looked outdoors again. "The window screen is like a canvas—no, an aqueous fabric with vertical lines of downward traveling water. Some drops stop midway, others descend like drops of translucent mercury. The newest and most prominent drips form slubs that look as though you could trace (yet not destroy) them with a fingertip. And through all this is visible a landscape of trees, branches bent low, and the white back porch railing, a bright geometric structure pointed like the prow of a boat into a watery world."

I've got to get out and explore! Pulling on a rain slicker, I dashed out the front door, and sloshed around admiring the uber-green of shiny wet leaves and the knitted look of the marsh reeds in the distance, blurred by drizzle and mist. So quickly did my sneakers get soaked, I might as well have gone barefoot in the first place. *I'm the only one out today . . . . Oh, how about the beach? I bet it's neat down there.* But then, unable to function with rain dripping into the shutter, my camera balked and I rejoined the company indoors.

My favorite solo moments of all, though, still occurred at night when everyone else was off in the little death of sleep. That was when the barefoot feeling translated to something beyond nakedness, an ability—always the desire, anyway—to clearly see myself and what I was dealing with. As though I could somehow x-ray myself by writing.

Remembering that hot August night when I unexpectedly "made a clean breast of it," I am reminded of Duchamp's famous *Nude Descending a Staircase*. I have always loved the overlapping states of the figure and the multiple exposure aspect of the painting. As though his impressions were too much for one static image, Duchamp conveys shifting states of mind, both internal and external. Yet motion itself, with steps forward and down, is the most important reality.

I see myself in that figure. A febrile, responsive soul full of ideas, now I had become the moving body who walked and wrote her way through life in the cottage. The barefoot girl was not just back but beginning to feel at home.

COUNTER SPACE

Channeled through two large windows, sunlight shines directly on a square section of counter between sink and stove. About twenty-four inches on a side, the surface is covered in gray sixties Formica patterned with little outlines of red and green boomerangs. Much necessary equipment lies close at hand, though not all is visible: can opener, silverware, knives, measuring spoons, faucets, and sponges.

This morning, a salad's in progress. A tomato awaits its date with the knife along with a wedge of lemon and one frilly leaf of lettuce which looks to have drifted down out of the air onto the cutting board. Like a reminder of the hours, a kitchen timer stands nearby.

This is home base: *the* place to cook. Located in the go-to spot opposite the refrigerator, the counter occupies a small fraction of a sprawling room about twelve by twenty feet with faded mint green walls and an uneven floor. The kitchen houses cooking appliances, pans, laundry machines, cleaning supplies, canned goods, bottles for recycling, toilet paper, paper towels, small appliances, a mess of paper bags, and a rack for wine. Flowers pass through, too; bunched on arrival, they get arranged in handsome old vases, then are later crammed into the wastebasket. The whole place speaks of multiple ownership, of people's tastes and needs, and "can't do without it" stands taken.

As for that section of counter space, any cook who inhabits a kitchen can identify such a locus: the sweet spot. Where you most often choose to work. Much like my favorite reading corner and the desk where I write, the home of my mind, that counter space is where I assemble raw materials and define my intentions. One of my prime creative spaces at Craigville, that spot is close to holy.

Consider another place of creation: artist Edward Gorey's home in Yarmouth Port, about ten miles from Craigville. Like our cottage, the place is a big weathered-shingle Cape Cod house, though built some decades earlier. For décor, think of Gorey's dark humor and eccentric style in a house. Since his death, the place has been cleared of most of his vast spread of possessions, except for the kitchen.

On the counter by the window, once the prime workspace in this kitchen, too, white tiles with dark grouting are barely visible under a sprawl of stuff: an English Brown Betty tea pot on a wooden trivet, an ironstone dinner plate, spheres of polished rock that look like dark plums, and brick-sized chunks of rock resembling cheese about to be grated. A footed compote holds marbles and grape-like beach pebbles. The compote is the lowest of three concave surfaces; the other two are composed of plates atop bowls. Everything is earth-colored, right down to assorted stones on the windowsills and shells in a pewter bowl. A little naked baby doll occupies a corner of one sill. Shrubs outside seem to peer in, their leaves shaped like eyes wide-open at Gorey's audacity.

A guide told me that Gorey assembled these items over some years while still managing to cook (barely); then he quit and left everything in place, petrifying the kitchen. While he rendered the room useless, he celebrated the cook as an ultimate decision-maker in charge of both food and composition of objects.

My first photos of his house were quick responses as I toured with friends; I was working hard to capture the visual feast. Only after a second visit and reviewing my photos from both times did I realize how Gorey's kitchen had affected me: the boldness of his stamp! Though he had created an anti-kitchen, Gorey's overall vision was clear; I had seen a place where someone lived a daily creative life in a Cape Cod house.

I cannot resist taking photos of food and the places and objects I encounter when cooking. When I press the shutter, I am saying, these things are real, tangible, edible, and soon gone. Apricots and pears with dots of water spangling their already sensual shapes. Or two images of peaches: slices glistening with juice, then the finished pie. I also take process photos, twenty-three images with the collective title, *Making Beach Plum Jelly*. Life and death pictures, too: lobsters before and after their turn in the pot. All revealed in the studio, the counter-top throne of the kitchen.

Still Life: Salad. In a round blue-purple bowl on the Formica, a concoction of chunks of tomato, sweet pepper, and cucumber. Primary colors, red, yellow, and blue flecked with cucumber skin and pepper and basil—bathed in light which transforms the bowl's rim into a wisp of halo.

    Garbage Photo No. 1. Over to the left, the trimmings from those vegetables—the salad's negative? Or perhaps we are being introduced to the in-laws and shirt-tail relatives. Crayon colors once again, this time against the white porcelain sink with a crescent-shaped slice of stainless-steel drain. Here are long dashes of cucumber peel as well as two breast-like ends, plus a couple of densely seeded inner columns, one rounded, the other triangular. A single divot of tomato (the stem end) and a yellow sweet pepper core studded with clumps of seeds. All of them in roughly geometric shapes, fallen in a composition like a Cubist painting.

Oh, that little square of counter space! I can write about that sweet spot but not hog or reserve it. I do, however, get grumpy if someone shoves aside a major set-up I have in place—and I am happiest cooking there with no one else around. As I work, I feel the space expanding to include the entire room, even the whole house. Steaming about kitchen and pantry, I select whatever I need, listening to Rachmaninoff all the while. From time to time, I check at the window to see if anyone has just driven in or is walking up the path. Cutting, chopping, and muttering to myself, I grab utensils from the drawers and slice and mix as though I were the only person alive. Salads, I place in the fridge to chill; I measure ingredients into bowls or bags and set pans and casserole dishes to bake. I am the captain on the bridge of my ship, creating wonderful things: at work in my territory, my vantage point, those four square feet of Formica counter.

Ears of Corn, No. 1. Pearly and gleaming, five shucked ears of corn destined for the pot. Each is an astonishing piece of creation. One ear, with the smallest kernels, is ivory-colored; the other four ears feature variegated kernels in white, yellow, and ivory. In spite of zealous scrubbing, a few threads of corn silk still cling on. Alongside, just off the counter, on the floor nearby, my niece's bare foot has somehow snuck into the picture and her toes match the kernels of corn.

Ears of Corn, No. 2. A close-up of two ears with a dark space between. Those scalloped edges look like a mouth whose pearly whites will bite! Each kernel swells and strains against its neighbor, with shreds of corn silk like tossed-aside dental floss. Or are the ears components of some weird machine about to roll around, gear-like, kernel to kernel? If dough were to be squeezed through, it would emerge puckered and cushion-embossed.

Garbage Photo No. 2. A bunch of leftover stuff. A faded orange sponge lurks behind a crumpled plastic bag. Alongside is a scrunch of aluminum foil whose edges have caught the sunlight. The facets glint! For contrast, off to one side, the back of a measuring teaspoon dull with age. In the background a plastic measuring cup with a spoon handle sticking up. The ghosts of cooking past.

At home in San Diego, I work at a similar section of counter, where my motion flows from left to right, from counter to sink. Every August, however, I fly east, where I chop from right to left toward the sink. Like Alice's reversal as she enters the "Looking Glass House," each existence is the same yet turned around, both familiar and different. To further complicate matters, I come to Craigville with a California viewpoint and a solitary cast of mind. Yet East or West Coast, no matter how much space I have or say I need, I gravitate to a patch that is about the area my body takes up on Earth. *This is where I fit.*

I have probably photographed that section of counter almost as many times as Monet painted haystacks. What uses will it be put to today? What transformations will take place? The views through the lens, and my memory, invest the place with drama.

Drama—and light. Specifically, morning light from an east window, Cape Cod light. Possessed of extraordinary clarity, on Cape Cod light expands space; so often I feel I have walked into a scene of creation and my mind has opened up so that I can do my own creating.

Still life, this time objects only. A bottle of orange-red dishwashing liquid labeled "cucumber melon" stands next to a small orange plastic colander. Sun-served, the colors glow warm and fiery; surely that bottle contains a magic elixir . . . .

Another morning on the Formica, three objects: a wire whisk with black rubber handle, a juice glass, and a discolored old teaspoon. Whisk and glass create complex shadows and the spoon stands by, the straight man of the group, as though to enhance the slanting right-hand line where sun falls off and dark takes over. The glass draws most attention; even empty and in need of washing, its elongated shadow extends forward in parallel arcs, making the glass grander than its actual self.

Taking over whatever lands on the counter, sun causes everything to look realer than real. Anything and everything is transformed, even the scuffed old Formica itself as it interacts with shadows, such as those of bumpy pears ripening. Or sun prints: pattern on pattern, when the designs etched on antique glass are cast over the little boomerang-shaped outlines.

Like me, Edward Gorey was a dedicated and incorrigible collector of objects. Why else do I keep a file called Things, and photograph the contents of the Craigville pantry? Stuff which people before me have assembled, such as multiple balls of twine and a package of those little toothpicks with crinkled cellophane at one end, used to hold sandwiches together in restaurants. And why did I photograph an old cardboard box printed *COCONUT PATTIES* but marked *6 sake cups*? Or tissue-thin petals of wilted gladiolus or a huge green pepper atop an overturned orange colander for a dais. A charming green-and-white spongeware pitcher I bought for the cottage, and shelves of dishes ranging from rosebud-patterned Limoges to discontinued airline china.

I collect them because, like Gorey, I treasure the variety of creation, the beauty of materials. We love each of these things for their roundness and roughness, their heft and color, and their uses and quirks. The camera makes it possible for my eyes to return and caress them over and over, and to collect in pixels and images as well as tangible objects.

Gorey, however, had the advantage of me. The house in Yarmouth Port was his, after all. He was famous and in charge of his life; I am anything but famous and cook as member of a shared household. In our summer camp of a cottage, everyone uses everything and everyone pretty much lives in every room. Viewing any location as mine alone is foolish.

Yet I grew up in a home with clear boundaries. One room was my mother's. Another mine. And then there was "Daddy's room in the basement" (or attic, depending on which house they lived in at any one time). Whether above or below, my father made himself personal kingdoms in those rooms. That was the settled order of things. At home in California, I am used to a personal workroom where I stash all sorts of stuff, write, edit photos, and make messes as I please: *my place.*

So how does someone like me fit into the Buffington orchestra of a family? Into the cottage?

Not only do I keep trying to live in a comfortable, nurturing relationship with other family members, but I also produce great dinners and birthday celebrations; I do laundry, help with closing for the winter; I entertain, come up with good ideas or remember some name everyone else has forgotten, or make connections that work. I keep the house going.

And I am a creative person in a shared place. I create simply because I cannot help it; I create to convince myself that this place is my home, too, even though I was not born into it. Creativity means feeling effective, coming up with lots of ideas, and writing and cooking and photographing all the time—the way I live in California—and the cottage is also a great and fertile place. Even as I chafe there, I sense this. I am drawn to that source of edge, that place where I feed on creative tension. Every summer I come back for more, back to that square of counter top. *My space.*

COLLECTED

*W*hen I went off to college, having never lived in a group setting for any length of time, I was always curious about other peoples' rooms. We all started with basic pastel-colored cells supplied with bed, desk, chair, and dresser. From September's crush of "How on earth will I stash all this stuff?" everyone's room progressed to May's settled state, each now its owner's signature space—only to get pulled apart at the start of summer.

However, going to Craigville, I met up with group space once again, this time in a shared summer place I could explore. Over time, I came to feel that the whole house functioned as a richly furnished room for the family.

Think of the old phrase, "If only these walls could talk!" At Craigville, they do. Walls or shelves or tables, bowls or travel souvenirs or utensils, just about everything comes with a virtual label, either a résumé-like history or messages in the form of adages that practically intone themselves. And all this forms a sort of breccia, as though the family identity is pressed together of everything in the house. In this collection of objects and items, everything possesses significance. Craigville has taught me to appreciate the power of objects and what they betoken or hold. *Study this place, Sally! It is a composite as rich as a pharaoh's tomb.*

You might start with a certain lamp. A homely old affair whose overall finish is an indeterminate brownish gray, the lamp probably dates from the 1930s or '40s. God only knows what color or finish it started out with. Five feet tall with a metal shade shaped like a quart-sized mixing bowl (and possessing all the charm of one), the lamp was once adjustable in height like a music stand. It turns on with a bead-pull chain.

One sticky evening, I wanted to read out on the porch where it was cool, so took my book and stretched out on the couch. I turned on the lamp. Nothing happened. On investigating, I found the lamp wasn't plugged in, so I did that. Now! I knew I had to pull the chain just the right amount. A couple of quick tries failed, so I attempted to work it by counting. Six beads' worth? Nope. I pulled a little farther. Eight beads, nine beads? Still no luck. Flashes of light, then dark again.

"Oh, damn!" After a few more ineffectual tries, I gave up and went back to read in the living room.

The next morning at breakfast, I reported the problem.

Andy said, "Oh, you didn't try to turn it on, did you?"

"Yes, but I couldn't make it work."

Pete added, "That's why I left it unplugged."

After some more volleys back and forth, I exclaimed, "Oh, for Heaven's sakes. Why can't we have something that normal people can make work? I'm going to just go out and buy something better and solve the problem!"

Later that morning, Andy and Pete went to the hardware store and bought a new pull chain assembly, which Andy installed. Now the lamp worked.

That repair took place several summers ago, and the lamp is still with us. Still ugly, still functional. And, much as I hate to admit this, it gives excellent bright reading light, thus lending the lamp yet more virtue in Andy's and Pete's eyes. For it illustrates the first clause of the old adage "Use it up/wear it out/make it do/do without"—and the third ("Make it do"), which is something of a religion in this house.

However, this adage comes with corollaries, one of which is "Save this, you might need it sometime." If you have saved it, good for you!

And just think! Someday, you may find even more ways it will help you make do.

For that, we have pantries, closets, cupboards, and an entire basement of stuff.

One mighty item reigns in the guest room closet upstairs: the Covo tin. Had I not married into this family, I might never have known that Covo was (and is) a shortening used in commercial baking. Decades ago, someone acquired a round tin drum whose prime feature, beside its large capacity (fifty pounds of Covo), is a very tight lid. In the days when blankets were generally made of wool, this impregnable container furnished prime moth-proof storage. A homely old yellowish affair perhaps twenty inches in diameter, the Covo tin is treasured; recently I heard Andy speak as though the thing were an architectural landmark or designed by some famous craftsman.

Another corollary to "Use it up," etc., is a label I sometimes come across: "Keep for parts." Opening a lumpy bag or wrapped oddity, I will find a disassembled old appliance or tool. Usually, the handwriting on the label will be Andy's, he being the local wizard who can repair almost anything. In the process, he often invents an intricate contraption a la Rube Goldberg. Such as the one where, had you come by that day, we would have said, "Watch out for the pile on the kitchen floor!"

Andy based the construction on two parallel bricks about six inches apart, on top of which a little white plastic spoon stuck out with bowl protruding; above this was a pile of four nested cast iron frying pans, all surmounted by an old yellow cane-seated chair.

Why the chair? To get your attention so you would not trip over the frying pans. Why all the pans? Cumulative weight. Why the plastic spoon? With the floor anything but level, it served as a shim to even the weight pressing on the glue. Why the whole contraption? Andy had set out to secure an old linoleum floor tile that had kept popping up, a perfect trip hazard right at the junction of the counter, pantry, dining-room, and refrigerator foot paths. Although he was pessimistic as to its long-term success, that assemblage got the job done. We have had no trouble with the tile ever since.

"Fix it."

Still, all this stuff. Sometimes I think these many things are here out of a thoroughness of living. Craigville is not just a summer cottage, it is a residence. Living there means not only fixing what needs fixing, but also having on hand what you need to do so.

"Save this, you might need it sometime."

Says who?

The voice of the house? Or the wisdom of some disembodied Yankee sage? Or is it the Buffington family soul trying to get through to a heedless Californian like me? I hear these inner voices when we are using or assessing an item—or, horror of horrors, when I suggest we throw something out.

All the old adages convey a reluctance to let anything go. Yet I also hear a sense of confidence lurking. "We can do it. You can do it. We are self-sufficient, we figure things out for ourselves."

Confidence, however, sometimes verges over into uppity boldness. After an especially heavy laundry day (four loads out to the clothesline and back), I thought, *You know, this old basket has had it.* With each load, at least a couple of its wicker strands seemed to break off and scratch me, plus one end had no handle. *No, I have had it.*

So I bought a new plastic basket, nicely curved to fit the sides of the body, with handles on all four sides and smooth, rounded surfaces. Pete put the old one down cellar. Though no one said this in so many words, I got the message: "Hey, we really needed that. I'm glad you stepped up. How bold of you!"

All that for $9.99. Ironically, I had found the thing on sale for college students outfitting dorm rooms. The price pleased this thrifty family. We don't need to be thrifty anymore, either, but as Mom used to say over and over, "You didn't grow up in the Depression!"

I got away with that purchase—but I have also gotten my comeuppance, more than once. *Watch out, kid, you're getting pushy . . . .*

Such as the new screen door for the porch. Andy and Pete had checked out local building supply places and finally found the right thing on sale. Jim happened to be visiting, so the Broze took off together to buy it. When they returned, empty-handed, I asked, "Well, where is it? Didn't you get it?"

"Nope—they wanted fifty bucks to deliver!"

"Oh, no! That one was exactly what we needed, and we don't have any other way to get it here—why not just pay and get the problem solved?"

"Nah, that's too much." Even though the store was over ten miles away and no one had a van or truck so we could transport it ourselves.

The framed message: "Old habits of thrift die hard."

Eventually, we somehow got the door, though I do not remember what delivery solution was found. My incredulous response has overtaken further memory.

All this is so personal. What is valued by one person is not, or is less so, by someone else. And in a place of shared decision making, this factor keeps popping up.

Yet people's choices and preferences also lead to the odd cumulative richness of the cottage. Unfortunately, however, the number of things has grown like Topsy and includes stuff from the older generation no one can bear to part with. People bring new plates and add them to the many already decorating the dining room wall. Every summer I rejoice in the lovely Imari bowl I got at a garage sale (a steal!), and Andy and I cannot resist yet more pottery from the studio in Dennis we admire. I wish I could take a baseball bat and smash that horrid china Fourth of July carousel that Pete is partial to; yet along with him, I treasure the Kimura pottery pieces he displays on the windowsill nearby.

"You can't take it with you." But that reality doesn't stop us. For what is really going on here, is endurance. "Hold onto it."

Or, "Don't miss this, it's oddly beautiful."

Then there's the dining room mantel piece. Or rather, the whole shebang, wall and mantel. Every summer, this becomes what Andy terms a "depository."

Here is what it looked like late in the summer of 2012.

The watercolor of shore birds, done by an artist Andy once met, was flanked by two mounted plates, one from Mom's and Dad's travels, and one that Andy and I contributed for its distinctive pattern.

On the mantel itself, over on the left, a jar of matches next to a flashlight—"You'll need these in case of a power failure!"—then paper napkins and plates, crowded in. Next, several small bowls, the first from a favorite potter, then two matching Japanese wooden ones. Quite the Japanese display, for next in line was a rectangular blue and white Imari sushi dish, plus a covered Imari pot full of yet more matches. Oh, and a dried sea star. Next to that was a little pipe-like object that I cannot identify, then two of the kind of thing that when you try to weed out, you never know what to do with. A gold shovel in a wooden-sided glass box, commemorating Mom's participation in ground-breaking for the retirement complex where she lived, and next to that, Pete's prize from a 2006 10K road race.

Frozen in time by my photograph—and memory—such inadvertent collages haunt me with their odd eloquence. The surface of my desk is another such display, as is also the living room mantel, and the old china cabinet in one corner of the dining room—and nearby, a bulletin board of numbers and business cards and thumbtacks, a tableau of Buffingtonism.

Remember these, save the memories. The records of this family and its times, traces of the lives they lived.

For all the things with a useful purpose, there are items without one— or that simply give delight. Nobody knows what to do with them—yet they are and always will be encrusted with memory and affection.

Like the monkey over the dining room table. Rattan, ten inches tall, it has hung by one arm from the Victorian light fixture for perhaps forty years. Eating a bunch of bananas, the monkey (pretty dusty by now) was a "What on earth can we get him?" gift Andy and I bought Dad for a birthday late in his life. Its offbeat whimsy and the surprise pleased him. Ever since, we have all relied on its being there. An "old friend" thing.

Save this, remember this. Each item is a piece of this place, just one part of a complex puzzle of a place I have helped create and maintain. A jointly created puzzle I love even as I dislike certain pieces or think their owners and defenders are nuts. All together, they compose a portrait of who we are, and who we were, in this place. *Save this, you need it.*

Remember this.

KURA

*O*ften when I think about Craigville, I bring up memories from out of a closet. An unglamorous old place, a bit musty, located in the downstairs bedroom.

Going in, I open the closet door. Straight ahead is a wire rack of the type usually found in a kitchen. About five feet high, its three shelves are loaded with dozens of old photo albums, folders, and papers. Some of the albums match, and most are labeled on their spines, some with cloth adhesive tape. For instance, "1956–62," or "Alaska Trip and Cottage." At one time, all the albums stood with spines upright, but sag and slant have set in.

Above the rack, Kodak Carousel projector boxes and dozens of long, dull-gray metal boxes of slides are piled almost to the ceiling; these stacks remain neat and undisturbed.

The closet might as well be a vault; throughout the chill of autumn, winter, and spring when the cottage is closed, it is one. Like a *kura*, which was a feature of the traditional Japanese house, though usually built separately, this is the Buffington storehouse of family treasure: our Craigville memories preserved in photographs.

After Mom died, the contents of the closet (which formerly had been kept in her apartment) sat around in cartons. No one wanted to tackle the job. However, because I collected antique photographs and had restored an album of Mom's ancestors that had fallen into disrepair, I began to look like a good candidate. Authorized by Pete and Andy, I eventually became the cottage archivist.

For a while after I had put everything in place, order prevailed. But with time and end-of-summer closing jobs, much unrelated stuff got crammed in, too, as well as clutter. In a way, though, even that random packing and mess related to the basic purpose of the closet. After all, memory itself is a messy and variegated affair.

However, the first archivist, Mom, had been anything but messy. In all those albums, she kept a thorough annual record: the family this summer, the scene (or many scenes) at the beach. Each picture came with a label, either printed in black ink or later a typed, pasted-in caption.

Following her lead, over the years not only I but also Andy, Pete, and Jo's (Joanna's) husband, Dean, have all made extensive collections of Craigville photos, though none as orderly as Mom's. My own files are a vast mixture, mostly unmounted, that includes both family lineups and more impressionistic takes on summer, the village, and Cape Cod itself. Often, I shuffle through my internal postcards and take an overview; equally often, I study a single image, for I am a pack rat and a collector who often imagines messages scrawled alongside or across the pictures. *Wish you were here.* Or *Look carefully at this one.* Many of my photos are not located in the closet-*kura*, but instead reside in computer memory back in California. Yet as I compare and remember, they fly to join those across the continent.

Family portraits take many forms. Take a formal example, a handsome professional enlargement from our daughter's wedding: the "whole fandamly." In it, the bridal couple is surrounded by about twenty relatives from various family branches, a mix typical of wedding groups. Though most of us are dressed up (for us, that is), we are hardly a formal bunch—and is so often true of such groups, we will never all meet again.

One place we do keep meeting is the front porch of the cottage, the ritual location for taking family pictures. Some people stand, some sit. The house is part of the group, as are pets: a squirmy hamster held by Jon, age eight, or beloved stuffed animals or blankies. All take their place. Not everyone is comfortable with the camera; some of our expressions possess all the loveliness of mug shots. For instance, in one front-porch picture, Pete looks downright suspicious and perhaps he was finding the place crowded that morning, though no one stood in front of him or stepped on his toes.

Other Buffington group portraits are less orthodox, such as one I call *The Lumpy Buffingtons.* I could have taken it any summer: a dozen or so pairs of men's socks on the clothesline, black and navy. Clothes-pinned up, all look like stretched-out prunes.

Yet in the background, all the whites—stair railings, window frames, sheets, pillowcases, and the clothesline itself—are straight and white as can be, as if somebody is trying to assert order on the place. Somehow.

And what of the cottage itself? Here's a view from the road below taken about 1907. At that time, the north end was differently configured; the kitchen devolved into yet another porch and the upper floor looked square and boxy indeed. Also, the cottage simply looked larger, perhaps

because the trees were sparse then. In sprawling script, someone has labeled the photo "Hillcrest," though none of us has ever called it that.

Adding to the "long ago and far away" feeling, the photograph itself is a double exposure, with faint trees and structures superimposed on bare sky. This feature gives a sense that the cottage is not as substantial as one might think. The spindly young trees surrounding it look rather like vertical tethers holding it to earth.

Then we come to *The Founders.* I don't know who took this portrait of Mom and Dad, Jim and Lois Buffington, who made the cottage into the place we all know, but every summer, originally at my behest, we display a framed enlargement on the mantelpiece in the living room to honor them.

At the time of the photo, probably the late 1970s, both Mom and Dad were in their seventies. As always, Dad looks calm, genial. He wears  a cream-colored sport jacket and striped tie. Beside him, in a bright yellow dress, Mom stands with her Leica and its leather case on a strap around her neck. Though smiling, she looks as though someone had said, "Let us take a picture of *you* this time!" Already she is raising the camera to have the next turn.

When I spoke with Andy about making the enlargement from the original three-by-five- inch print, he replied, "Well, first we crop it, right?"

Though I usually agree with this strategy—close focus on faces—this time I said, "No, I think the sense of their bodies is important. Let's see them whole."

Another day, a sequence of pictures of tree trimming. A bunch of us crane our necks at a scraggly tall Douglas fir in the front yard. A big branch has been dangling and Anne's husband, Mark, has volunteered to climb up and lop it off. In the first picture, Anne watches apprehensively; in the next two, Andy and Pete evince supervisory airs. Next image, Mark himself so entwined in branches that I find it difficult to locate, let alone focus on him. Next, returned to earth, he looks hot, also relieved. Click. Here are Pete and Dean discussing what to do next. Click. A keepsake portrait of three beautiful fir cones that fell, then one of Anne's back as she raises binoculars to follow a bird. Final image: Pete and Dean, saw and sawhorse; the branch, now chopped up, is about to join other drying logs awaiting their turn in the fireplace.

A view out the bedroom window: the white railings of the back porch and the parallels of the empty clothesline seen at an angle through faint soft parallels of screen. The clothesline is a spider web. Or are its white strands harp strings?

A view taken in the downstairs bedroom, looking into the bathroom. Beside the door, a blue-and-white Japanese bowl sits on a small table. Seen through the doorway, flowered curtains flutter in the breeze; above the toilet hang a pair of old framed pen and ink sketches from "somewhere in the Orient." A faint green light emanates from walls and woodwork, all of it in temple-like verticals: the old cross-and-Bible door, moldings, door frame, paneling, and wooden molding that covers the wire from a wall lamp to the floor. An aura is present, even a hint of the mystical.

Leafing back through the albums, or just looking at a single image, I feel a sense of ghosts, of the people who are not present. One summer's day Andy and Pete stand on the front step, another day all three brothers. Another year, our older daughter, soon due to give birth, did not come; that summer her sister stood on the front step with Andy and me. All of us were anticipating the baby, Andy's and my first grandchild, a then-unborn spirit we searched to discern in the dim outlines of a sonogram photo. If that image and all our talk about it could have made him real, he might already have been born.

We handle snapshots, bring up any image we wish on our computer screens, or take yet another digital photo. We go through albums. Or we send or receive a picture in an email or on cell phone or by Facebook: whatever we have captured and changed into image existence. Yet for all the richness I draw from them, photographs are as insubstantial as waves dashing the shore.

At the same time, though, we succeed at freezing moments. On a morning walk, I photographed a tree sharply outlined in the shallow water of a puddle, knowing that the moisture would soon evaporate—and I possess the image. As well as one of a drying green oak leaf on the doorstep that reminded me of a juvenile dragon, briefly come to rest before flying off again.

Or I think of my photograph of a photograph: Pete with his camera aimed at Rowan in the front yard. The baby from the sonogram, now a toddler, playing with water in cups and bowls and pouring it over himself. Pete and I had the same intent, to preserve that stage of Rowan's growing up. The moment as quickly gone as the water absorbed by the ground where Rowan was playing. The real subject? Youth and age, one generation watching the next.

Or one of my favorite images from later that same summer: Andy had just delivered a punch line to his old friend Carl, whose face has crumpled into laughter. A split-second along their decades of friendship.

Whenever we study all the portraits and images, momentarily we, and they, become real again. The images live as postcards to our future selves. Someday, photographs may be all we have to go on, to remember this place, its surroundings and people. Images we can pore over and cling to, evidence of how we have loved this place, and how it has figured in our lives.

Among many others in my computer archives, I have assembled a file called "Craigville House." It includes pictures of all four sides of the house, some taken in daylight, some in dark, and in all kinds of weather. Also an image of the watercolor painted by neighbor Marty Sherman of the cottage in snow, a sight most of us never see. Thus, I can compare the "Hillcrest" image of 1907 to a recent one taken from the same angle in fresh sunlight. How much more substantial the house looks now! How colorful, too, with the state and college flags Pete hangs from the porch railing, seen as you come up the path.

Or how about my rainy-day photo, taken through the car window from the same vantage point of the 1907 photo. This one suggests my annual last-look-back when I leave. As its automatic setting often dictates, my camera focused close-up so the raindrops registered in crystal-sharp focus; everything else, especially the house, is blurred. In the gray day, even this color photo looks rather like the hundred-year-old one, though a cheery light shines in the kitchen window, and leaves and grass are summer green.

We do not see through the proverbial "glass darkly" here, yet in that image the cottage seems distant, as though receding or fading. It is also so flat-on a view of that one side that the picture seems like painted scenery, a reminder of the way the cottage offers us all a stage set to act on every summer.

Someday, however, the archive in the closet will be dismantled, dispersed, and located somewhere else. I fantasize that even if the cottage were to fly apart, the closet would somehow remain intact, swirling off into the sky in *Wizard of Oz* fashion. And somehow as it flew, we could still reach up for guy wires or halyards and bring it and the contents down for consultation, any time.

As long as we go there, we keep putting images in, rather like Japanese *ukiyo-e* prints, "pictures of the floating world," of scenes that have existed here. All these pictures in our *kura*, and the *kura* itself, are our defense against the passage of time and mortality: the memory house within the cottage.

However much I want them, there will always be photographs I cannot or do not manage to take or think of taking at the time. Some emotional knowledge will be forever closed to me; I can never get it all. At times I have gone to the closet late at night and pulled out an album at random, reading its pages, inhaling long and deeply, as though I could somehow draw out the essence of this family.

Yet I also view a given photo as something like a pebble cast in a pond; my response causes the ripple to widen and grow . . . and then disappear.

Every image is a tiny piece of Craigville and captures something we want to hold onto. Sometimes I can preserve only in mind, like a vision of the marsh before I went to bed one night: a subdued halfmoon of light shimmering on steel gray ripples, a Japanese print. Or, as Andy said of one photo that we agreed had not worked, "The camera doesn't see as your mind sees." Sometimes words do better to gather just the right details of an ambience or conversation. Or, unobtrusive though I try to be, my camera imposes itself and spontaneity is lost. I am left to remember as best I can, trying to imprint the incident until I can later record what I manage to remember. My take on it, whatever that turns out to be.

Yet another contribution to the contents of the *kura* in my heart.

PERSONIFYING

Should you come into my cottage office and look around, you would see a couch, a table piled with books and papers, and back to your right, an open closet door revealing old photo albums and boxes. Oh, yes, the *kura*.

However, straight ahead of you, is the desk. Your eye is drawn there, and right away you could be pardoned for thinking something like, *What a mess! . . . I don't see how Sally can work there, it's so crowded. That desk is small enough as it is . . . . Why she does she have all these things—old portraits, it appears—cluttering up her workspace? They don't resemble anyone in this family, and they're brown and old, antiquated . . . . Why not display portraits of her daughters and those darling grandchildren instead?*

Who are those people anyway?

Over many years, I have accumulated a huge collection of images, real, remembered, and virtual, that I consult and work from: a personal *kura* that accompanies me wherever I am. This group on the desk is a tiny subset of my collection of antique portraits. All of them are people I do not know, portraits I have bought because I responded to the faces. I am attracted to a subject's personality, the vividness or fineness of an image, but more than anything else because I wonder what this person has to tell me.

The images are printed on sepia-toned cabinet cards (four by eight inches) or *cartes de visite* (two by three inches), a form of photographic reproduction popular around the world from 1870 through 1920. Often the photographer's name and location are supplied (usually stamped or embossed at the bottom or printed on the back side), but seldom are any clues provided as to the subject's identity; even so, such inscriptions as "Aunt Minnie" or "Cousin Ralph's son Samuel, age three" do not convey much. I am left to read their faces and if I want, to compose group portraits like this one on the desk.

When I found the two young men's portrait in an antique shop, I responded immediately. *Say, they're rather like Andy and Pete. . . at home together—a unit, even . . . .* The two women, I bought at different times, then compared later. *Oh, the younger one, is she perhaps "me"? Her portrait is rather like my "betrothal" photo when I became engaged to Andy back in 1968 . . . . Is this darker-haired woman a more mature Sally?*

And then. *Oh, yes, now here's a redoubtable soul! . . . Is that you, Mom?*

At first, I just casually laid them out. *Hmm, that makes an interesting group.* I let the portraits work on me. *If I listen, I might hear their voices . . . . Something is going on here . . . .*

Allow me to introduce you more personally.

This young woman is one of thousands whose portraits were taken at the brink of womanhood, all over the United States. Like

so many of her sisters, she wears her hair piled on her head and is probably in her severe best dress, usually black or dark colored. The printing technique has caused her to appear in sharp relief, almost as though sculpted. A serious soul, she appears to be trying to see the future; I also sense that she is much concerned with manners and propriety.

The second "me" (who is not related and lived in another state) is probably twenty years older. She appears to look at

the world carefully, yet with appreciation; she considers all the possibilities. Somehow, I intuit in her a quiet sense of humor, also that she processes her experiences and thoughts much as I do. She knows herself.

Both women exhibit a heroine-like quality that greatly appeals to me—and might well supply the way I saw and still see myself at Craigville.

And here are its young men.

On the left, "Andy," and on the right, "Pete," as they might have appeared in the early 1900s. I have no idea who these pictured men were, nor whether they were brothers. I also see no family resemblance, but then I do not see much physical resemblance between Andy and Pete, either.

What I do discern is their bond. Though these two are just starting out in life (they cannot be much over college age), I often see Andy and Pete the same way, as brothers who are friends; together they feel like their ideal selves, ardent, verbose, and genial. The portrait reminds me of when I first knew them both, ready to face the world together. The Broze United.

Perhaps lumping together the Pete and Andy I know diminishes each separately—or does it, as with a married couple, create another entity, a joined personality? I can also report that the Andy of Andy/ and/Pete is a somewhat different person from who he is at home, independently.

In recent years, these two men I live with are alternately delightful company—and sometimes companions mainly to each other. I notice a sweetness to their relationship, especially when they reminisce or relax over a single malt. Their photo also reminds me how often I think, *They've never really grown up.*

And now: Mom.

Appropriately enough, this photograph is inscribed: "Daddy's mother, Nellie Ryan, March 28th, 1912." Yes, someone else's mother-in-law. While Andy's mother looked nothing like this battle-ax (a label he himself applied to the portrait), somehow this face conveys more than a little of how I found Mom, and still do.

This woman! Nellie Ryan doesn't meet you halfway. Proud and strong, she is someone you present yourself to; not a woman as a supporter, but a woman as a challenge. Also, if you cover Nellie

Ryan's fur collar and plumed hat with your hand, the face revealed is masculine—and formidable. *Well, that fits.* As the only woman among Dad and the three boys, Mom acted executively; her intelligence and vigor deserved far more outlet than running a household. While Andy and Pete do not agree, I have long felt outrage that Mom never used her journalist's training after she married; I feel that she pushed herself and the rest of us with that thwarted, "masculine" energy.

However, Mom was also a lively, fun soul indeed, both in person and in her letters. Yet this antique portrait presents a reproving personage whose silent voice says, "Well, we never did it that way." Or reminds me, "Aren't you going to finish the dishes?" Or even, "Don't forget that leftover zucchini soup in the refrigerator, it needs using up!" And sometimes, "Think *this* way, the way I do." I bridled at that, as well as the force with which Mom delivered her opinions.

So here they all are on my desk. Under my control. Personified as I have chosen. I can move them around and focus long and hard on any one or create a sub-group at whim.

Sometimes I think, *How distinguished we all look! Maybe we'll all seem this way to the descendants someday, too . . . . Hard to believe right now, though . . . . And how formal! None of us ever gets this dressed up these days.*

Or putting the others aside, I give Mom pride of place. Solo. I glance over and think, *Well, you can't get at me now, Mom, and I can control the way I think of you . . . .* At such times I imagine her answering back, with asperity. *Oh, now wait a minute, Sally. Someday you'll be dead, too, and pictures might be the only way* your memory *lives on.*

Ironically, her image is the only one of the group whose back side is printed for use as a postcard, a feature sometimes offered by photographers of that time; Nellie Ryan never got sent. I "send" her now in the form of my reaction, and thus keep her alive.

I have long since given myself license to portray and characterize. And to declare that I am the one who matters here. Mom's equal. Holding Mom in portrait form, I talk back to her freely, even put her in her place. Have I got the upper hand? These printed pieces of cardboard represent both the hand I was dealt and more importantly now, the hand I have dealt myself.

At the same time, I might ask, *Isn't all I'm doing pretending? This is self-indulgence, Sally, kid stuff. You're using these photos as adult paper dolls and dressing them not in clothes but in imagined attributes.* Perhaps the qualities I assign to each face amount to little more than stereotypes.

Yet doing so allows me to posit and dream as I wish; I feel no requirement to be just or kind or forgiving. The faces cannot talk back, let alone correct me.

With time for only a glance, I take in a kind of visual tincture, or sip an elixir; after careful repeated study, I drink a tumbler-full of their substances. Either dosage is powerful. As with perfume, whatever the degree of strength, their substances were, and still are, potent and evocative.

My desk display shows not only that I collect antique photographs, but how I draw inspiration from them, and how they play a role in my creative work. The observer with her own visions, I am a kind of Louisa May Alcott of the Buffingtons, the interpreter of the family, who also keeps learning yet more about herself.

Using the portraits represents standing back from the situation to understand it—and is a sign of confidence. Though I cannot actually possess Mom or Andy or Pete, I possess suggestive, allusive portraits that stand in for them. And I celebrate myself as a complex personage who watches and takes an overview. While I would never have predicted this when I first bought the portraits or brought them together, I have become the author of this family's narrative as well as my own birth story. I have adopted myself in.

TREE HOUSE

*A*s the years of summer rolled on, I began to look harder than ever at the cottage itself. What did Craigville have to teach me, and where in its reaches could I find myself? I studied the house from top to bottom and kept trying to separate out family history from my own thoughts, trying to see things for what I thought they were. To learn this place.

A typical August morning, six o'clock. I awaken in Andy's and my room, in the upper northeast corner of the old wooden house. A bright, narrow rectangle of sunlight frames the windows as the dark green shades slap lightly against sills and sides. I slide out of bed and pad over to pull them up.

More light rushes in, filtered through fir and oak trees whose branches brush the roof. To the north, I glance out over the lawn and marsh, trees and rooftops, then return and settle back down next to Andy's warm body.

Both of us yawn luxuriantly and gaze up at the ceiling, the knothole eye above, and the islands of wood grain. Under all those narrow slats of board, I feel like a mouse who's found a cozy home inside a rolltop desk. At the same time, the sheets are pleasantly cool as they drape my arms and legs. Before some major linen replacements a few years back, though, I often awakened in the dark, trying to stay covered with tattered strips of aged percale.

Caw! Caw! The crow chorus. Oh, of course, creatures who have lived in and around the house for years. Until Andy and Pete filled some open cavities under the roof in our room, I often heard bats. From the homeowner's point of view, they were anything but desirable; yet I found their dry sounds oddly charming, as though someone were scratching away at a manuscript with a balky quill pen. And way back, raccoons nested in the downstairs fireplace one winter and left behind a mess of damage; squirrels once settled in the ceiling above the kitchen. Though all those entrances are sealed off now, their stories keep getting told, so in a way the critters are still with us.

Looking around, I muse that Andy's and my room is anything but four walls and a ceiling—instead it's a complex polyhedron, and an irregular one at that. I count eleven different non-horizontals, including the slanted roof angles I encounter when I make the bed or reach to turn on the light near our bureau, which is itself squeezed into a corner and angled in by the sloping roof. Slanted walls are typical in the other upstairs rooms, too; to make the far side of Pete's bed (and get around those high bed posts), I have to positively contort myself. Each summer I consult my body memory and do it again, much as I know by feel and height where to grab the light string in our closet so I can undress in the dark without waking Andy.

Highlighted by sun, against the soft yellow walls, a few dust motes drift about and, in my sleepy state, seem like traces of past summers. I think back on tired but joyous arrivals late at night and all our unpackings for yet another visit. I remember that incredible thunderstorm one summer night at 3 a.m. that banged everyone awake except our little daughter.

Many of the memories floating around here connect me with Buffington history, like the banged-up old fishing rods above our bed that belonged to Andy as a kid. I keep my books in a little hanging wall shelf Jim made in junior high shop class. And all those family stories! Including the lovely tale of Dad's warming the three boys' clothes for the day on the downstairs fire screen when they came down for chilly fall weekends so long ago. Tales of disasters, too: Dad's fall from the roof, and my visit on crutches after an accident back in 1986, when Mom kindly gave up her bed so I could I sleep downstairs. I hug to myself all kinds of memories: the kids shucking corn with Uncle Peter, Anne bushwhacking her trails, my love of sitting among the trees and bushes, and my ongoing search for Indian pipe, that odd plant that sometimes pokes up through damp leaves a day or two after rain. The trees surround and arch over the house as though embracing it.

By now, sun has filled the room and all the leaves are chlorophylled-out with fresh yellow green. The trees themselves seem bushier and fuller.

Time to get breakfast and take on the day.

Aha! Do I smell bacon and coffee? Nope, wishful thinking. I'm the one to get breakfast going.

And even if Mom were still here and cooking—she always got up before anyone else— Andy and I would have been rousted out long ago. I would already have contended with the dresser across the room whose drawers stick unless you pull the handles equally, yet sometimes they stick anyway. Already I would also have checked to see if the bathroom is free.

From across the hall, I hear a mattress creak. Sound carries through single-board uninsulated walls. Pete's voice. "Anybody awake around here?"

At Craigville, there is no room, no window upstairs or down, from which you cannot see trees: we see through a glass greenly. Or we experience wood in some form. Going upstairs is almost like climbing nailed-down planks up a tree trunk to a platform above. Big though it is, the house offers a feeling of escape from the real world. You are free, at home yet somehow outdoors inside and safely harbored, anchored— or becalmed—in a world of leaves, branches, and trunks. With the sun's rays diffused and spread by leaves, the house is an environment of pattern-filtered light and sudden brief solar-graphics, in irregular shapes and patches. Light on the lawn around us, and on the roof, is always dappled.

Is the cottage a "treehouse" or just a house in the trees? A real treehouse is a fantasy place, a construction hardly anchored in earth and built for children, or adults with a fanciful bent. You go there to play without care or responsibility, to a place removed from normal life. A treehouse is a place where you make things up, where you improvise.

On the other hand, sometimes being at Craigville is like walking through a forest where the trees have grown too close together. I know who is sneezing or coughing on the other side of the wall. All too well, I remember my embarrassment in early married days when I came down to breakfast, wondering who had heard Andy's and my springs creaking in the old cast iron bed in our room. Yet years later, one of the younger generation asked me, "How do you ever have sex in that house?" Andy's and my room is desirable exactly because it has the only really comfortable double bed.

Then there is the intercourse, so to speak, of getting along with everyone. For many years, Mom was the trunk around and from whom we all branched. Since her death, no one person is in charge of the cottage and we function as a committee—inefficiently but more democratically. Everyone's branches and twigs rub at times, their roots get kicked and trodden upon. Sometimes I go out on limbs.

In this house of family ties and rubs, I revel in being part of the place, and in being a member of the family tree. Craigville is some of all of these things, and at the same time, a homestead. Our house in the trees keeps giving life, a framework for belonging and lasting through good times and bad. And the trees around us, their limbs branching out protectively, bless us as they murmur "There, there . . . ."

CEILINGS

*I*f asked to choose one feature of all the wood in and around our treehouse, I have to name the ceilings. Wherever I look upward (except in the kitchen and bathrooms), my eyes roam a vast variety of wood. Originally lightly stained, tempered by time, those cottage ceilings are made of a material known as beadboard. It is wood for which the word "glow" was invented, wood that comes alive in light, revealing all sorts of shades—russet, amber, chestnut, and umber, gold, caramel, and cinnamon brown.

This rich color spectrum is rivaled by the multitude of patterns in the beadboard. Patterns in woodgrain, knotholes, whorls; all kinds of parallel lines, from close, almost-touching strokes like those in old engravings, streaks and stripes, all the way to irregular, almost blistery contour shapes . . . like elongated islands on long, long maps . . . ripples forming and reforming in tide pools . . . no, oil spreading on water . . . pools of pigment spreading and sinking into thirsty paper . . . a marking that flows all the way across the room, as though creating a narrow stream bed . . . here, a little bend in the grain . . . and the markings on this plank are like embroidered threads . . . . Here, did the tree shiver or tremble in the wind decades ago . . . or did it feel and radiate waves of sun-warmed health and growth?

All these features became a source of imagining and fantasy for me, starting every morning with the knothole of eye watching over Andy's and my bed. After saluting the first morning I awoke there every summer, every day I silently hailed it once again.

Though most people interpret this as a sign of boredom, at Craigville, staring at the ceilings is an intelligent response. I am reminded of the "Touch with your eyes" admonition that I hear parents give children in antique shops.

Beadboard is a building material of narrow tongue-in-groove planks that appear lined up with a ridge (the "bead") between each board. The antique wood in the cottage ceilings is probably cypress. A millwork product, beadboard enjoyed great popularity at the turn of the twentieth century and was often used in summer houses and cottages. Some of our neighbors at Craigville have also used beadboard, though most of the time they have painted it white or a pastel color, which is why every summer Andy would admonish me, "Don't ever paint those ceilings! You'll *never* get them back!" Recently, village friends commented, "Oh, you've kept the natural wood!" The clear implication was that our cottage had remained true to the original spirit and use.

One day I carried out a personal survey. Moving from room to room with pad, pen, and camera, lying flat on beds or couches, I relived an Armstrong television commercial from my teen years: "Ceiling Watchers, Look Up!"

It went on to boast, "Master craftsmen made a ceiling worth looking at."

Oh, yes!

Some boards had been cut from the same tree or section of trunk, yet each panel was almost as individual as a fingerprint. At the same time, whole ceilings appeared like vast ocean surfaces from which some long-hidden creature might issue forth. Yet all these beautiful and suggestive designs marked parallel boards laid out straight and narrow, whose shivery grain lines reminded me of the tissue-like markings on slices of agate . . . no, tiger stripes. Another patch brought to mind the patterns of snakeskin. And oh, no—for just a moment a gaping mouth on one plank suggested Munch's *The Scream.*

I even began to wonder if all the patterns amounted to an assemblage of the cottage's EKGs, as though all our beating hearts had thus registered over and over throughout the years.

More than anything else, though, what all this wood evokes for me is music. Especially with the lights on, the combined effect is of a benign, tawny harmony. In the living room, the ceiling, augmented by the staircase, possesses a mix of foxy hues that resemble the surfaces of cellos and violins; the overall blend of color and pattern calls up the harmony of Beethoven string quartets or Smetana's *The Moldau,* that musical portrait of the great river flowing through his Bohemian homeland.

Yet the instruments most often played at Craigville in my time have been woodwinds. Early on, my silver flute, but my dominant impression is of our dear friend Carl playing the oboe, with Andy at the old upright piano. By preference, the guys played Bach, but also Handel, Telemann, Vivaldi, and Andy's own compositions.

Whenever Carl played the oboe, his balding head shiny in the light and reed pressed between his lips, his face soon turned red. His pupils responded to the black note heads traveling over the pages of music on his stand. Andy, anchored to the old piano stool, would sway from side to side, his fingers ranging over the piano keyboard, left hand never stopping though his right turned or smoothed down pages. At especially high notes, Carl's eyebrows rose up his forehead, while his fingertips pulsed on the silver rings and keywork of the slim black woodwind.

Stopping for breath or between sections of the music, the two would play on and on. Andy's line might surge forward as Carl sustained a long note, or Carl would take up a ribbon of Bach and interlace his melody with Andy's. In and out, above and below, their lines of notes interwove in feasts of Bach and friendship, transforming the wooden reaches of the cottage into a kind of local cathedral.

B.ASEMENT

*A*t the back corner of the house, diagonally opposite to where you arrive, is an old white door with a square window. Grab the handle, noting the Andrew-Wyeth– worthy flaking paint and worn steel of the plate beneath, then depress the latch and open the door. Step right in—and take a deep breath. Elixir of cellar: a combination of earth, concrete, spider webs, dust, wood, oil, rust, rope, paint, turpentine, rags, and God only knows what else. A rich fragrance indeed and appropriately so, it introduces a place of defining and carrying out purposes, and "the right tool for the job."

Though my province is largely upstairs, I always come to the basement with reverence and affection; I come to plumb photographic riches, to locate the Broze, and to further understand this family's adage-driven life. Also, though the walls are concrete blocks and the floor poured concrete, I always feel close to the earth down here. Sometimes I go in just for the smell, happily reminiscent of my father's workspaces.

Whatever the reason, I feel a major sense of possibility: "You can solve any problem if you're willing to work at it." The basement is a place from which you manage life.

Take a couple of steps farther. In this subdued light, the rest of the world recedes behind you. No matter what the temperature outside, it is always cool here. Looking around, you see lots of things, including some that make you wonder what they are or do. The longer you gaze, the more you see. Take your time. This place is (or should be) anti-hurry. Keep looking around, above, below, and beside you. Your eye is drawn to multiple objects, drill bits in graduated (or not so-graduated) sizes, screwdrivers, pairs of pliers, and seven different hammers: a collection of American hardware of the last seven or so decades. Labels on the containers stake their claims: *Mends old leaks, prevents new ones.* Or *Stops rust . . . Protective coating . . . Seal-It Pipe joint cement.* All sorts of bits and pieces are stored in old Skippy and Heinz and Hellman's jars.

This is a people place, and a museum of house. With the exception of spiders and their webs, everything is covered with fingerprints. In its way, both space and contents, this place—the basement—is the mind of the cottage.

We all depend on this room, about twenty by thirty feet, which anchors the house on the hillside; the basement walls supply the foundation as well as being the bottom story. The basement is corporation yard and workshop, project base, the flesh and blood of the Red Notebook, and a clinic that cares for the cottage's ills. Should you need them, over in a cubby you'll find Band Aids, adhesive tape, and antiseptic. The air holds silent echoes of banged thumbs, muttered curses, effortful grunts, and reassuring thumps on the back.

An awful lot of plain old stuff has found a home here. The banged-up old laundry basket with only one handle, the deacon's bench with an arm that needs mending, dozens of lengths of leftover wood, old coffee cans, and paint brushes that any other family would have long since discarded. Some things are of course vital, such as stepladders whose drip-stippled steps record all the paint colors used in the cottage over the decades.

Besides shelves with their array of labeled glass jars, the pegboard's holes and hooks anchor tools. A few drawers are attached to the workbench that runs along one wall. Oh, and a jelly cabinet: homemade, painted the dark green of the cottage's outside trim, with screening on three sides for ventilation, this is a square box about twenty inches tall. None of us makes preserves anymore, but this never stopped Pete from shoving in a few empties with the accolade, "That'll make a good jelly jar." And for some unknown reason, a string of fancy porch lanterns has also gotten stuffed into the cabinet.

Need a rake? Over by the door. Butterfly or fishing nets? Up in the rafters, along with lengths of old doweling and baseboard. Need a bucket? What size? We have several. Extension cords, wire, rope, sawhorses, calipers, sandpaper? We have 'em all.

However, so much down here is "out of sight, out of mind." Maybe that is a luxury of life, to just stash stuff willy-nilly and some distant day come back and examine it as though you are an archeologist divining what early settlers used these objects for. An image of the plethora of objects might be used for one of those multi-thousand-piece jigsaw puzzles: all those intricate gadgets and their wood-metal-earth color range.

Down here, people get defensive and take stands. "Save this, you might need it!" One summer morning, my eye fell upon an old whiskbroom whose normal five or six inches of usable bristle below the stitched binding were worn down to barely an inch; any brushing capability was limited in the extreme.

Andy was explaining something so I waited until he had finished, then pointed to the whiskbroom. "I think we can ditch this, don't you?"

"Hmm? What?"

I handed him the truncated broom. "You can't brush anything with this!"

"Oh, but have you got another?"

"I'm sure we do —but I mean, this isn't even worth keeping!"

"Are they still being made?"

"Oh, for Heaven's sakes! A whiskbroom? It's a common item!"

"Well, don't throw it out yet!"

Later I took the old thing upstairs into the house and photographed it, then bought another the next day and dumped the antique in the trash.

Now it has lodged in my mind as a symbol: in this family of practical doers, the whiskbroom was equipment from their laboratory and I was not acting in the correct spirit, even posing a threat. That whiskbroom was a piece of "us." Normally, Andy would have said, "Pitch the damn thing!"

These days most people have neither the time nor inclination to work at all these jobs; instead, they call a handyman or buy a new whatever-it-is. The Buffingtons are different.

Though Mom and Dad bought the cottage as an already-built entity, they kept on building and working at it all the years they lived there, and Andy and Pete and niece Jo and her husband, Dean, have continued with the practice. Built-in New England independence, a philosophy of life with principles and resources you can depend on. A philosophy you pass on to the next generation.

In a way, the basement *is* the cottage. It is also a repository, and a palimpsest. Musty, also dusty, it is a place of history on which the Buffington family has written over and over: a temple to "Do It Yourself."

UNDER ALL

A straight shot out the front door, right before I went out to the yard or turned down the path to the road, there it was: the bendy board in the porch floor. With every step in just the right place, I felt a little give, just a bit of spring. I loved the way it felt, so much so that sometimes I did it several times in a row.

However, the more down-to-earth part of me recognized that board as symptom of a problem. This was Red Notebook stuff, part and parcel of the family's stewardship of the cottage via home repair. The entire porch floor—all the porches, surrounding over half the cottage (except for the newly built platform off the back of the kitchen), needed redoing. Ever since 1906, all these porches had done double duty, tramped over every summer and weathered by damp, salty air all the rest of the year.

So one September, instead of closing the cottage, we left it open for an excellent carpenter, Don Tarr, to live in while working. However, before flying home to California, Andy and I went by to check on his progress and found the place in an odd state indeed. Don had removed the entire porch floor; only the roof and sides remained in place. No more bendy board!

Now we could see the support system, though "system" appeared a generous term for all those miscellaneous pillars of piled-up bricks or hunks of old trees. One looked like cedar, about two feet tall and four inches in diameter. Another larger trunk section four-and-a-half feet tall had been used on the downslope side. Compared to a modern foundation, the old house did not rest on much of anything, especially our beloved screened porch, which appeared to have depended on chunks and stumps for support all these years.

Andy and I went prowling around, and he showed me the place that made him most nervous: the northwest corner. He pointed at the vertical four-by-four, then poked into the wood. The first section of his index finger disappeared.

"Good Heavens! What's in there?" I asked.

"Who knows? Could be dry rot, or—"

"Can we do something about it? I mean, what can Don do?"

Andy outlined several solutions, including a complete rebuild of that section above as well as below. I asked if we could just fill the hole, as we fill concrete slabs and cracks in California if a main piece is still sound.

"Dunno. We have to depend on Don's expertise here." Accidentally, Andy brushed against another "pillar," and that section of old tree trunk dropped out onto the sloping ground, straight toward my bare toes. I hopped aside. Off it rolled into the woods.

"Well, I'm stumped!" The two of us dissolved into laughter. Stumped indeed.

But problems underfoot went deeper still. This replacement job had started with yet another redo—the cottage's septic system. When we sought permits for porch reconstruction, the town informed us that we could not proceed until we had taken care of the septic.

Like it or not, we were in for a siege of a kind. But for me, the whole set of processes turned out to be unexpectedly rewarding—and to answer a long-buried question. As the work went on, the phrase *Under all is the land* kept flashing in my mind. What did that mean?

I had first encountered those words way back, in ads for the real estate office where my father worked when I was a teenager. Oh, that euphonious flow of *l*'s and *a*'s! Sounded attractive, but I didn't get it. So I shelved the quotation in my mind along with all the other grownup pronouncements that might get explained, someday, sometime. I later learned that *Under all is the land* is the first sentence of the Code of Ethics of the National Association of Real Estate Boards.

The words surfaced again on a sunny July morning. From around the garage, a huge yellow backhoe growled across the lawn below the dining room, a trapezoid of grassy slope perhaps forty feet across. Having positioned itself and dipped its toothed scoop downward, the monster bit through grass and dirt as though both were soft as marshmallow. Chomp! Roar! Hmm, I thought, *the local version ought to be "Under all is the sand"*. . . . But not white beach sand. As with most of Cape Cod, sand means orangey-brown soil with a texture like brown sugar.

At first, my elevated section of porch had seemed like a perfect grandstand seat. But then I thought, *I've got to get closer. This is fascinating!* And threatening. When the backhoe scraped and fractured the concrete of the walk, I felt as if I had seen someone's ankle crushed.

"Someone's ankle . . . ." *It's just concrete, not human flesh, Sally . . . . You're taking this personally.*

I rushed down to join Andy and Pete on what remained of the upper lawn. We were all caught up watching, though only the engineer got down and dirty by jumping into one of the holes and guiding the digging operation.

Whenever there was a break, the driver dragged on a cigarette. At one point the backhoe lost traction and its right rear wheel began to spin. The engineer yelled out, "Willy, wait!" and grabbed two fair-sized stones from near the garage and thrust them into position under the wheel. The machine shuddered back from idling, then got a purchase on the solid rocks. Off it went again, marauding like a dinosaur, squashing twigs and bushes and bending saplings.

The aim of this dig was what is known as a perc test, to determine the best place for the new septic system. Once the holes (eight feet deep) had been scooped out, an engineer placed a perforated bucket in the sand and poured in water. If it seeped easily into the ground, the theory went, future wastewater would also readily percolate into and through a leach field located there.

Leaning as far over the edge as we dared, all of us peered into the first hole. Four big red cans, twenty-five gallons of water, disappeared in about four minutes. Good, this one passed. (Anything less than fifteen minutes was okay.) A little while later, the holes in the woods also passed.

Hmm . . . you really know you own a place when you get mesmerized by its septic affairs.

A few days before, Andy, Pete, and I had walked the entire property with the engineer's topographical map in hand. Surveyor's stakes with pink plastic flags marked the edge of wetlands, the marsh we must protect, and blue-flagged markers denoted the presence of existing water pipes. The old cesspool, however, needed no identification. I remembered when a guest once asked, "Where's that smell coming from?" I knew all too well.

As for less grungy landmarks, I had always wondered about the faint traces of something more than a path in the woods near the point. But until Pete explained that day, I had not known that it was a road used in harvesting marsh hay, a resource back in the nineteenth century. I also learned about the sharp drop-off at the edge of our lawn. Now covered with vines and ending at the tidal river, it was the site of yet another harvest, this one of sand. Those early Cape Codders used the land hard, almost to the point of mining it. Preserving the thready-looking green marsh would have seemed to them an extravagant, romantic notion.

Yet getting ready for the dig, we had done one job those early settlers knew well. A higgledy-piggledy bunch of rocks, hardly a wall, bordered our path, getting in the way of what would later be the third and fourth holes. Andy crow-barred up the bigger stones, and Pete and I rolled them downhill a few feet. Using a size-based hierarchy, Andy then stacked them by the side of the garage. I called the big ones *hams*, the medium-sized, *baked potatoes* (*fillers*, in Pete's term), and the leftovers, *meatballs*. In the process I gained great respect for those lengthy stone fences I have admired when driving Route 6A in Cape Cod towns like Yarmouth and Barnstable. Our burdens were light indeed.

Moving the rocks, we exposed a thin layer of chocolate-hued topsoil that gave off a concentrated earthy smell, like the leafy humus I had breathed when walking in the woods. Then Pete and Andy went to work on seedlings behind the garage while I acted as trash-pile go-fer. I liked the feel of wood on my palms as I carried it, especially the bouncy branches of a cherry sapling.

In the process, we also turned up worms and a large, flat chunk of pitted concrete that Pete said was "part of Aunt Annie's walkway." I had of course heard of that grande dame who sold the cottage to Andy and Pete's parents decades ago; she gave no special terms because they were related or because they had two small children with another on the way in a few months. And before their time, Aunt Annie had gotten into a boundary dispute with the neighbor whose land abutted our walkway. He erected a spite fence so close that no one could walk past our front porch, so she had the corner of the house cut off just enough to make space for a Buffington-only sidewalk. Today, with the fence long since removed, this section of porch is still blunt-cornered, but the roof juts out in a point over the walkway, as though thumbing its nose at that long-ago neighbor.

Wow, she must have been a flinty soul! We ought to have a figurehead made for that corner whose lips hiss, "Don't Mess with Us". . . . A possessor, for sure . . . . But perhaps Aunt Annie loved the place, too, in her own odd way. Or was she simply defensive of her property rights?

As we talked with the engineer and local health officer, a host of unfamiliar terms came up. The house needed help. *This is like dealing with someone's health emergency and trying to suddenly understand all the medical jargon and make the right decisions.* Siblings, cousins, uncles, nieces, and in-laws, we were gathered 'round the old dowager; sometimes we agreed—and sometimes not.

Though the town's requirement of redoing the septic at this point caused endless grousing on the part of the brothers, I was relieved; I felt it should have been updated long before. I also hoped we would leave few or no marks, and that all our work and investment would respect our location next to a salt marsh. Nevertheless, even with the best technology available, I wondered, too, if someone fifty or a hundred years hence would regard *us* as benighted and alter or disable this new system, as we were doing now with the old cesspool.

Up to that "summer of the septic," I had just lived in the cottage, taking for granted its permanence and concentrating on my own domestic and creative work. Yet often unconsciously, I was amassing a private claim on the place, accumulated of layers of experience. This included a green and white vision of the screen porch, also such remembered sounds as wind swishing through the trees or the music of voices in dinner table talk, the roar of a heavily loaded dishwasher, and Andy playing hymns on the piano in the living room. I knew and loved how it felt to open the front door first thing every morning and check out the day's marsh view; I also loved choosing which old platter to use for one of my creations from the kitchen. My claim held its tactile aspects, too, such as pulling sheets taut against my fingertips when I made beds or navigating uneven ground under foot when I took loads to the compost. Over and over, I had walked all around the cottage, over grass or compacted dirt, or the uneven old path stones. The details of my claim changed with every day's experiences, even moment by moment.

As for the cottage itself, it claims the land lightly. When you face the front door, it appears to just *sit*, as though someone has deposited a big, wide box. For real evidence of its stability, you have to look at the other three sides. Then you see how the cellar secures the house as it nests into the side of our small hill.

And what about the land, our piece of the intrinsic place that is Cape Cod, long before the Buffingtons or anyone else ever came along?

The Cape first emerged out from under formative glaciers tens of thousands of years ago. Much later, native Americans of the Wampanoag tribe arrived; some of their descendants live there still. Subsequently, in the 1600s, English settlers came to Cape Cod. Craigville is a village within Centerville, itself a part of the town of Barnstable, where mostly white people used the land in the early 1800s. The nearby beach where we swim was for many decades a busy harbor used by fishermen, shipbuilders, and seafarers. As for our actual property, it is part of a subdivision from 1872 that carved beautiful acreage into miniscule rectangular slices for summer tent camping in a Christian revival settlement. An antique map on our dining room wall documents the layout; later many of these slices were combined into patchworks of parcels.

Today our house at Craigville is part of what I call "metropolitan" Cape Cod, with both summer and year-round residents gathered around the city of Hyannis, itself classed by the census as an "urban area" of fourteen thousand people. In summer that number swells vastly.

I find it endearing how people hold summer places and make them into shrines of the mind. On our whole crowded planet, though most of us cannot afford more than a tiny patch of earth, we attach ourselves and look to the land to anchor us. Our Craigville, the cottage we so love, is just one of thousands.

At one point, soon after the septic job was finished, I wrote, "I see the history of our cottage as like the ground beneath it, composed of layers. We have settled here, cleared patches of land, moved rooms up on our hillside, and placed our boundaries; yet all we really own are our lives and stories, the strata of words and steps, deeds, and family trees. As the years go on, the leaves fall and fall again, decaying into the sandy soil. Rocks collect; pebbles, shells, and bones compact into the dirt. Leaf by leaf, year by year, Cape Cod lives on. Every summer, we move upon it for a time. Under all, the land lives on."

A romantic overview. Yet ultimately, I saw that like everyone else, this family and I were subject to mortality; all our work and lives would never leave a lasting mark. Caught up as we were in caring for the cottage, perhaps only "dust to dust" would end up connecting us to the earth.

As for the bendy board, it has long since perished in some landfill; the "new" septic system is now over a decade old and invisibly working away, thank goodness. I look back and wonder why that dig, that seeming violation of the front yard, stirred me so. And why should I remember that yielding board in the porch floor?

I think now that both were part of an unlikely rite of passage. They reached me because they were so physical, even visceral. Beyond illuminating that enduring slogan, the board was giving me a message from the house: *Pay attention, Sally. No matter how time-consuming and annoying and family-argumentative this place seems to you, no matter how seemingly mundane, you are connected here. You are part of me. No longer a kid floating on the efforts of others or playing with an old board, you are an adult now. You must take care of what you love—and to do so fully means feelings its ills and needs as you do those of your own body.*

No longer a girl on Cape Cod, I was learning this place and my grown-up woman's part in it in all my senses—and all its senses—as they revealed themselves in wood or reeds or rock or earth.

COMPANION

*I*n childhood years, I used to go out behind my grandmother's house in Newton, Massachusetts, through and beyond the lawn and garden, to the place I thought of as "out-in-the-woods." Once there, stepping over roots that seemed like the earth's bones, I followed paths of hardened earth. I climbed a favorite tree and surveyed the hillside and neighborhood and, one amazing day, saw a scarlet tanager in its branches.

Sometime during those years, I learned that a man named Thoreau had lived out in the forest in Concord (about thirty miles away) about a hundred years before. A cabin in the woods: what a wonderful and natural idea! I knew no more than that about Thoreau but thought that he probably liked scuffing through oak leaves as he went, just as I did, hearing them crunch and rustle and sniffing the dusty smell.

When I was eleven, I moved to Cape Cod, where nearly every day I walked the shores of Minister's Pond in Eastham, a wooded landscape little different from Thoreau's Walden shores. And throughout my teenage years, though not consciously thinking about him, I kept going out around my pond; I loved being alone there. Nature embraced me. In those moments, I felt myself a member of the family of the woods. At home.

Over the decades that followed, I lived comfortably with this naive "man who lived in the woods" concept of Thoreau. Though assigned to read some parts of *Walden* in American Lit., somehow the book barely registered; I was too busy then making my way in the fascinating world of a conservatory of music. Interestingly, though, my musician friends and I referred to our solo time in practice rooms as "woodshedding."

Years later, as an adult, I found myself going to Craigville every summer, and there I finally came to know Thoreau. For in 1995, on the verge of turning fifty, I read *Walden* for the first time.

A serious reader, I not only loved the natural world but nature writing and memoir. Given these tastes and my quest to become a writer, *Walden* of course had been nudging at me. I was also constantly journaling and working to know myself better; how much more classic or American soul of a guide could I wish for? Not surprisingly, *Walden's* effect on me brought Thoreau's words to life: "How many a man has dated a new era in his life from the reading of a book! . . . which will explain our miracles and reveal new ones."

The copy I read came with a Craigville connection, though it had made its way to our California bookcase. A version published in 1946, the front endpaper bore the inscription: *For Leslie . . . to be read in our own Walden . . . from "me."* This meant Mr. Leslie Swain and his wife Anna, friends of the Buffingtons who had retired to a woodsy cottage in Craigville; their copy came into Andy's hands when they later closed out that house.

At first, I was startled by Thoreau's combative tone, as though he had leaped up on a convenient stump and started lecturing. *Calm down, Henry, get off your soap box!* Soon, however, Thoreau wormed his way into my thoughts—and *Walden* has worked on me ever since as a slow burn. Or to put it more gracefully, I have come to consider *Walden* as a river flowing through my life, replete with tributaries; at various times, some particular chapter or paragraph surprises or washes over me—or seeps in anew.

I do not always march to Thoreau's drummer. Often I find him opinionated, even pompous, also full of allusions and sometimes (to me) obscure references. In addition, I have not adopted his ideas about material goods, both because I live among a prosperous family that enjoys such things and because I enjoy them myself.

Always, however, I am inspired by Thoreau to search out my own path; I have always felt vindicated by him that such searching is the way to live. No matter what other forces influence me, no matter how much I do or don't accomplish, I feel, as did he, that "my head is an organ for burrowing . . . and with it, I would mine and burrow my way."

In the summer of 2000, I found myself at Craigville with an unexpected kind of millennial independence, freed to start living what might be viewed as a second adolescence: simultaneously a growing up and a conversion. Over the past year, both my mother and mother-in-law had died; I was almost through the menopause; and my daughters had finished college and were out in the world—all this as I had been working my way into writing.

Now, like Thoreau, I want to give "a simple and sincere account" of how I lived in those years and to understand what I learned. While I have never experienced what Thoreau famously described as "a life of quiet desperation"—I have always possessed far too much spiritual faith and general optimism—I have always felt there is more ahead that I must seek. And even though I was living every summer among good people at Craigville, in a place that oddly came to function as my Walden, what I valued most is what I did via my own exertions and what I learned from them.

However, living at Craigville meant coming to terms with "the morning work in this world," as Thoreau put it. What exactly should I do with my days, especially those prime hours after breakfast? What about the housework that my mother-in-law had so zealously done, "when the furniture of my mind was all undusted still"? At the cottage, I myself supplied the home-cooked meals that Thoreau's mother served. My existence was complex indeed, balanced between loving familiarity, my in-law status, and my own purposes.

What deserved my attention first? How to put my own house in order? Laying in necessary equipment, I bought a copy of *Walden* to keep at the cottage. Now, whichever coast I found myself on, I could consult Thoreau and feel as though I were receiving his messages.

Before he ever built his cabin, Thoreau himself owned a tent and used it near Walden Pond "when making excursions in the summer." He wrote that its "frame . . . was a sort of crystallization around me, and reacted upon the builder." My inner frame existed within a shared family place; Thoreau's cabin was just a mile and a half away from the homestead. We both sparked off family, depended on them—and defined ourselves against them. I was living out the realization that *Walden* is not just by and about a man who goes and lives alone in the woods, but a man in relation to people.

The distance I traveled to get to our cottage made for a concentration of mind that magnified each summer's experience—and each visit returned me to a source of self that I could find nowhere else. Not only had Craigville become a stage set of a kind, but also it was located on Cape Cod, a primary place against which I value and test ideas.

Thoreau and I shared the circumstance of repeated visits to Cape Cod; unlike me, however, he never lived there. During his four trips between 1849 and 1857, it truly was the "wild, rank place" he called it, with little or no resemblance to today's summer paradise. I have read his *Cape Cod* several times, though it is very different from *Walden*.

It too has marked me with a famous phrase. Neatly capturing its outline on a map, Thoreau described Cape Cod as "the bared and bended arm of Massachusetts." When asked about Cape Cod, or where our cottage is, in response (and I have seen others do this, too), I instinctively extend an arm, bend at the elbow with my fingers curved in, then point with the other hand to where Craigville is located. For that moment, I am part of Cape Cod, body and soul—and it becomes part of me.

Down the front lawn from the cottage, going toward the marsh, I look for a slight opening in the trees. As I slip through, foliage strokes my forearms as though clothing them with sleeves.

Except for bird calls, it is quiet here. The path before me wends its way across a gentle slope covered in oak leaves. At a stout tree, I pause and trace the bark with my fingertips. A substantial branch extends out toward the marsh, and where it bends away from the main trunk the bark bulges as though the tree were flexing a muscle. A few steps farther and I join a vertical community of trunk poles and dowel-smooth seedlings, some with encrusted rings or bands of growth. Just ahead I spot a young pine whose needles sway in the breeze like anemones bending with underwater currents.

A catbird flits about in the bushes, a nuthatch heads down a tree trunk. Squirrels fling themselves over the branchy freeways. I brush midges from my face; then, looking down, spot a rustic pancake with fork-tine edges, a mushroom served up as though Martha Stewart had positioned the oak leaf on top. Another 'shroom, caved in at the center, is handsomely garnished with twigs; alongside, a multihued leaf hints at fall ahead, as do dry, curling vine leaves that resemble violin scrolls.

From this shelter, I see the cottage only dimly. The house is reduced to lurking. Someone might call me from the porch, but visually I have withdrawn: I am "so near and yet so far." Thus unnoticed, I am free to explore the natural world in detail. Or, as Thoreau put it, to "transact some private business with the fewest obstacles."

I also walk in the village of Craigville, though one afternoon, a bush-choked entrance to a trail almost deterred me. But just as I was thinking, *Hell, I'll live with poison ivy if I have to*, a broad flat path opened up.

From there on out, it was as though I swam upright, using occasional breast strokes to deflect a branch or vine. Walking a composted pad of leafy carpet, my every step released an earthy bouquet. Alongside, it looked as though rustic embroiderers had been at work. A few pine needles lay across velvety mini-pincushions—cast aside once their creators had made those round moss pillows? I came upon star-shaped bursts of Christmasy green, broccoli-like clusters of light blue-green, mosses embellished with gray-white threads of lichen, and tangled bundles of sage-green thread, as well as branches and twigs frilled with ruffly fungus.

Reaching a copse of ferns suffused with sunlight, I sat down on a log and took a deep breath of sweet blossoms. My bare arms luxuriated in warmth as my eyes touched a black-and-yellow beetle, then the finger-shadow of a fern on a yellow leaf. Oh . . . a handsome hawk-like bird on a branch . . . . Was this the young osprey I had seen around the marsh and once in the backyard? Yes! Centering in with the zoom lens, I inspected him more closely than ever before—and captured his image.

When I walk, photographic possessiveness takes me over, sometimes approaching a picture per stride, though of course images do not occur at anything like that measured pace. On sighting something arresting, I enter a yoga-like photo salutation: inhale, gather thought, focus, press shutter, exhale. In the process I become the camera alive.

Even without a camera, I focus photographically. One summer morning, coming on a particularly fresh young sapling, I visually disregarded everything around it, as though reducing all else to blurry background. *I'm turning into a lens.*

What if Thoreau had had a camera? He was photographed himself (that famous 1856 portrait of a homely man with homely whiskers) but lived before ordinary people used cameras. Instead, he carried with him equipment that his friend and writing contemporary Emerson detailed as "an old music-book to press plants; in his pocket, his diary and pencil, a spy-glass for birds, and a microscope."

Thoreau and I capture and hold images selectively. Out of hundreds, even thousands, of possible impressions, our eyes center down on this perfect blossom or that leaf so meticulously spotted it might have been engraved; we rejoice in a berry-laden sprig of juniper or a branching shadow-print of foliage on the ground. As Thoreau might also have done, I mentally entwine myself with vines spiraling round a stem or splay out my fingers like fern fronds toward the sun. Bending down, I read the sky in murky reflections in swamp or pond water or palm the ground to impress my own pattern.

My observation and learning are aided by something else Thoreau probably never foresaw: the computer. With it I write, process, and view my own photographs, study information and thousands of available images; I record data and communicate with others. Yet I think of Thoreau as the embodiment of an interior and rather romantic super-computer, with all his powers of observation and synthesis.

He and I also draw upon the emotional technology known as personal memory. Often in surprising ways, it responds to situations and ideas and makes use of sensory input less conventional than the books and botanical drawings that Thoreau knew or made himself, or my books and journals and files. For me, memory endows all kinds of specimens with suggestive, reminiscent patterns or images.

For instance, consider a ring I wear featuring a flat, oval slice of labradorite, which recalls a long-ago experience. On a blustery March day, I was taking a bus from Springfield, Massachusetts, to Boston. Mile after dreary mile, we barreled along the Massachusetts Turnpike while rain poured down from a lowering sky. Rusty-leafed oak trees drooped over an endless succession of hills.

After a half hour or so, with no explanation, the bus stopped in a rest area for twenty minutes. Staring out the window through the streaming drops, I thought, *I wish I could get out!* I longed to shove the door open and leave everything behind and rush into the woods. I wanted to run and run until I could not be seen, palm-slapping tree trunks as I flew past, and hide under a bush or overhang and sit in the woods. Alone.

Instead, I waited for the bus to start again.

Cold and wet notwithstanding, sodden and gloomy though they were that day, those woods were ground of a kind I knew intimately. Thoreau would have recognized them, too: Massachusetts woods. There they were in front of me—and I could not return.

Yet, in imagination, I have. For the stone in my ring presents an image much like those woods. Vertical striations in the labradorite resemble tree trunks, themselves crossed by a diagonal reminiscent of a New England stone fence, a diagonal like a path that leads me. In some lights, the dominant color of the stone is blurry drab brown. Yet when held just right, the lines reappear and immediately evoke that landscape. Whenever I wear the ring, I go back there.

I have also imagined for myself a specimen of Craigvillite: a composite of oak leaves, pine needles, fungus, spiral-curling vines, toadstools, pebbles, and tuffets of moss, with cherry-red dashes of sumac tossed in.

I have always been fascinated with memory, especially the question of why we remember what we remember, but my fervent camera use is a phenomenon of a little over a decade. During that time, though, being able to preserve what I see and instantly or later review has come to seem almost equal in blessing to the generosity of nature itself. Over and over, image begets image. For this reason, I sometimes think of photography as a sixth sense that takes observation and memory and builds upon them. Or is it a seventh, with memory itself as the sixth? Either way, my appreciation and sensory love of nature has flourished with a camera as never before. In particular, bark of all kinds makes me marvel at the fingers "of the Artist who made the world," in Thoreau's words. Trees themselves, I see as an endless variety of sculptures, and their branches ink the sky in kinetic calligraphy.

Or, aiming the camera at the ground, I capture a patch of earth. For instance, one laden with shapes and cut-out embroideries of decay (an insect's meal) on curling leaves. Another patch, a few steps away, offers a collage of twigs, acorns, fungus, white quartz pebbles, and miniature fir cones. Sometimes I am rewarded by an animal presence, such as the thumbnail-sized toad I once spotted in undergrowth near another Massachusetts pond.

I am never totally alone in the woods. As Thoreau himself put it, there I am in the "presence of something kindred to me"—an embowering place where I feel complete, where my thoughts have time to unfold and form and compose.

But what about society? How do I live day to day with the family around me? What about that "bouncing off" idea I have mentioned?

Once again I think of the "tent frame" Thoreau described as "a sort of crystallization around me." No matter how many people happen to be around, I remain alone within the frame of myself. I think, write, photograph, and walk, keeping a pad open on the table next to my bed, pen alongside, ready for whatever comes to mind. If I cannot record something at a particular moment, I mentally jot it down.

Still, I am not always comfortable. As I wrote one summer, "It isn't just 'nice' to be alone, I desperately need it. As always, I'm adjusting (not gracefully) to the groupness of Craigville, which was of course intense this past weekend . . . and I expected things to be this way, was quite prepared . . . . But the adjustment is greater this year than ever before—I am so used to My Home. Alone . . . . I'm grumpier."

Another summer. "Being here is a test, a balancing act. A joy, a curse . . . and a challenge."

I have found myself at the cottage, or clarified my thinking, in private defiance. *Hell, I'm not letting that talk stop me. What do I think? Okay, Sally, define yourself.* And off I go with pen or on foot. I argue on the page and make my declarations of intent, then act on them. The people I live with are an audience I both want and do not want.

I have also argued for a more generous point of view of the cottage itself. One instance was the infamous (in my mind, anyway) porch table discussion.

Long before I ever came, Dad constructed pull-up tables along the side overlooking the marsh; we have used them over and over, as that porch, with its views, is one of the loveliest places on earth. However, with more than three or four people on hand, this creates a lineup and gives the impression that we Buffingtons have turned our backs on the world. Talking in a line has never stopped *us*—but how about pleasant, face-to-face conversation with guests or friends on a beautiful summer evening?

So I suggested to Pete and Andy that we buy a rectangular table for the porch.

I might as well as have suggested installing a Sherman tank. Or a roller coaster. Both guys burst into outraged cries of "We've never done it that way" and "There's not enough space."

I suggested a collapsible table, "Oh, but where are you gonna store it? We haven't got enough storage space *any*where."

I explained that I would buy a table that was as portable and collapsible as a card table.

"Where you gonna put that?"

"With the other card tables in the corner of the bedroom over there, there's room for it, Pete. I've checked already."

"But what will it look like?"

"Well, it's a casual folding table, you don't expect great furniture. Besides, I'll use a pretty tablecloth and you'll never see what's underneath anyway."

On and on they went, with question after suspicious question, until I gave up.

Yet I have opened up this society, often with Andy's support. Both of us were eager to make up for Mom's final years, when, due to her age and declining energies, we could not entertain more than the occasional approved dinner guest. Freed to act on our own, we quickly invited friends and relatives to come and encouraged our daughters to do so, too.

To me, the cottage is more than Family. Craigville is a privilege and benison—and should be shared. In effect I can make the cottage larger by including in more people and ideas, though not as casually as Thoreau, who sometimes returned home from a jaunt and found people waiting at his cabin.

Already I loved to cook and share food, so that felt natural. But more than food, we would hear new ideas, laugh at different jokes, play more chamber music, or share simple friendliness. Back in the wedding summer, we entertained not only many people new to us but also local friends; in turn we were invited to their homes. The occasions we offered ranged from simple suppers to Pete's "Whiskey Tea" for a village elder to an evening that seems in retrospect like a progressive dinner in our own house, so helter-skelter were the arrivals of guests and more guests, along with repeated runs to the pantry and fridge for yet more food.

Our gatherings began to spread out over all the porches or chats by the barbecue, and many styles of talk obtained. Thoreau himself might well have lurked in the shadows watching, so trenchant were some of his observations. "If we are merely loquacious and loud talkers, then we can afford to stand very near together, cheek by jowl, and feel each other's breath; but if we speak reservedly and thoughtfully, we want to be farther apart, that all animal heat and moisture may have a chance to evaporate." He must have been thinking ahead to the Broze.

Friends have brought their dogs; their kids have played with the cottage stash of toys. I have put on many birthday celebrations, whose candle-laden cakes offer a symbol: a light of fun and welcome, a lantern almost. For Craigville is a gift that I came into by no plan or action on my part beyond marrying Andy. I want to deserve it, which means I must keep on giving and sharing it.

If this sounds sentimental, so be it. For it is a role I can and must play in this society: the agent of welcome, of opening the place up. The one whose inner cabin of happiness and self is reflected in the place where she resides.

Though Thoreau never formally offered such gatherings, let alone birthday cakes with candles, he received people in his cabin; he was also familiar with his mother's (Cynthia Thoreau's) generous spirit and shelter to escaping slaves, as well as her "in the woods" son coming back for home-cooked dinners. She, Henry, and I are openers-up of thought and welcome; we are the light-givers.

Still, I am familiar with times when any light I offer shines for me only.

Sometimes The Family matters; I do not. I noted one evening, "The constant assumption of their concerns, their companionship, their noisy arguing and talk over projects. I can and do stand up for myself, but eventually I get tired and discouraged. Or disgusted."

Then, heeding the words of yet another American, Mark Twain, I "strike out for the territory." I leave and take a walk, seized by something like a physical need to be alone, to immerse myself in myself. I even hide from local people I encounter; more than once on walks have I crouched behind a bush or shrub to avoid someone.

And later, I retrace those steps. Via photographs, in the cottage or at home. I zoom in, contemplate, and compare. I relive these walks much as I think Thoreau did while sitting in his cabin or swimming in moonlight. As he wrote in the beginning of his chapter "Solitude," "This is a delicious evening, when the whole body is one sense, and imbibes delight through every pore. I go and come with a strange liberty in Nature, a part of herself." He speaks also of "a long evening in which many thoughts had time to take root and unfold themselves."

Henry David Thoreau always invites me in, and his words continue to offer the hospitality of the cabin "out in the woods." I carry *Walden* within myself.

OUT LOUD

August 2011, Mattakeese Wharf, a Cape Cod harborside restaurant, a favorite in our family. That day, the place offered a scrubbed-clean Cape Cod view: rippling water, bobbing boats, white sand, puffs of clouds, and a soft, salty breeze blowing in through open windows.

The four of us around the table, however—Pete, Andy, our niece Jo (the business manager of the cottage), and I—looked anything but beautiful. *Yup, we're the rumply bumply Buffingtons!* The guys wore frayed or paint-stained old khakis, and Jo was in her usual summer combo of tank top and cargo pants. For me, white slacks and a bright T-shirt.

We ordered food, plus beers for Andy and Jo, and a Coke for me. Pete went for a pomegranate berry martini, which turned out to be a pretty pink drink in a martini glass. Looking pleased, he offered us all a sample.

Handing it back, Jo said, "Oh, that just tastes like a mix of Robitussin and Vodka!" and wrinkled her nose.

"Hmm, nice, Pete, sort of a party drink!" I said after my sip.

Now for lunch: fried clams, scallops, fish tacos, chowder, and French fries, delivered to whoever had ordered them. Even so, with all that on hand, after a few minutes I thought, *I hadn't known this was to be a family meeting, but it's beginning to feel like one.* Much legal and business stuff about the cottage, plus the ever-fertile subjects of plumbing and repairs; I had heard it all before so listened intermittently and kept enjoying the view.

Finally, though, a break. *Well, maybe this is a good time. We've all relaxed and it's good to have everyone together.*

"Hey, guys, can I get a word in? Pete, can you put the newspaper away, please, for a moment?" Grudgingly, he crammed it into his tote bag. "I want to let you all know that I'm starting in to write a book about the cottage. It'll be a personal memoir."

"Oh."

"Yeah?"

They resumed. "Well, now, the fuse box job got done the same year we had those new toilets and the shower installed, right?"

Andy answered, "Yes, and that's all worked out really well, hasn't it?"

Oh, for Heaven's sakes! I've heard all this fifty times. And they just rolled over what I had to say . . . . Well, I'll try again. Wait for a better opening, too.

Jo chimed in. "But we need to be building up our funds. You know, the roof's not going to last forever!"

"Too soon, Jo. Besides, the roof's holding up pretty well, and we just got through those biggies, the septic and the porch." Andy chomped down on another fried clam.

"Besides, who you gonna get to do it? There's always that problem," Pete put in.

"Oh, you know," Andy said. "We'll get recommendations, the way we always do, interview people, you know the drill. And we'll find someone—but then we gotta supervise 'em."

After twenty minutes or so, and seeing that everyone had finished eating, I spoke up again. "I brought something up earlier and I'd like to come back to it. It seems to be hard to claim your attention." Andy sighed, but I forged ahead. "I want it to be known, I'm serious about this book. I'm working on it with an advisor. I love the cottage and I want to write my take on it, even though I know I'm a non-owner, an outsider."

Pete, seldom so acerbic, said, "Maybe you ought to pay rent."

Wow, that was a cheap shot.

Jo pulled herself back from what she was about to say and turned to me. "Why do you think we need to know this?"

I wasn't expecting that. "Well, because I live with you all much of the time, I mean, I want to get along with everyone and not cause problems." Pete nodded. "Also," I said, "you might have questions— and I want you all to know you can ask me anytime." *Seems to me like acting with basic honesty. These people are involved in what I'm doing, I'm hardly going to spring it on them.*

Pete spoke up. "Will your book be like *The Big House*?" Referring to an excellent memoir about another Cape Cod family summer home.

"Pete, I've read that one—it's really good—but I'm not writing the same book at all, even though I respect Colt's work."

Jo added that her husband Dean had long felt himself in the same non-owner situation that I was and that he, too, deeply cared for the cottage.

"I know, Jo, I mean, I can tell he loves it—all those photos he took!"

Well, maybe I can get in one more point here . . . . It's always seemed to me that creative work deserves to be celebrated or at least taken some account of. Rather than a "Why's she bothering us with this?" kind of reaction. "It's rather an honor that someone writes something like this, you know!"

During all this, Andy had stayed silent, watching with a furrowed brow and finishing off his beer. *I wonder if he wishes I hadn't made this stand at all. Or is he giving me space, and letting me handle it myself?*

Then the next impersonal topic bobbed up and off they sailed again on home repairs. *Oh, dear. I guess my speaking up was just a distraction. Well, at least I've done it . . . . I tried to speak calmly and without excess emotion, which is vital to making points around here. Didn't embarrass anybody, I think . . . . Well, I'm not put off. I am going to write this book. But I sure do feel like the odd man out.*

Andy knew I kept a journal and that I had written essays about our lives at the cottage and how I viewed the place, but I think the rest of the family had pretty much forgotten my big piece for Mom back in 1993 (*All the Years of Summer*), though perhaps not the booklet of essays about Craigville I had circulated in 2008, or my trio of poems in memory of Judy (*When I Sing*) in 2010.

My announcement was a declaration: "I am a creative woman, more than just the friendly domestic manager you have all become used to who's nice to have around now that Mom's gone. What's more, I am going to make myself a particular position of my own here and prove it by writing a book."

I was speaking to very practical people whose reactions usually ran along the lines of "Well, you never know with statements like that. Show me the money."

In time, their reactions that day came to work on me as a goad. *Okay, I'll show 'em!*

Later, in small ways, the Buffingtons did endorse or at least recognize my work, but most of the time, I went ahead without recognition or support. Which might also be viewed as free rein.

How or where did I get the idea of a book about the cottage? Certainly it built on the short collection of pieces about Craigville I wrote after Judy's death. I think now, however, that its true origin lay in an unexpected vision, some years before even that.

One August morning, I had gone with Andy to a rehearsal at the home of some Craigville neighbors. We played and sang for a good while, then everyone packed up to leave. As our host, Ed Deyton, took us to the door, I caught a glimpse of brilliant color in a room we passed, also the sheen of silk.

When I asked, Ed replied, "Oh, that's a quilt made by a relative of my wife—would you like to see it?"

"I'd love to!"

He took us into a sitting room whose primary decorative feature was a crazy quilt in a large (eight by ten feet) gold shadow-box style frame. It was (and still is) probably the most perfect such one I have ever seen.

Without thinking, I blurted out, "That's my memoir!"

Ed, Andy, and indeed I, paused. I laughed nervously, every sense on alert. At my enthusiastic comments, Ed told us some about the quilt; I asked if I could come back and study it carefully, and also photograph this amazing thing.

"Of course. When would you like to come?"

When I went, I sat a long time thinking and looking. A gifted woman had taken many disparate pieces and created a tight, balanced whole, which was displayed within double outer "frames" of fabric, one of ruffled purple taffeta, then plain black. Then the quilt itself began in earnest, edged in a rectangular frame of squares of striped fabric, each one different from its sister. This frame enclosed a kind of blocky spiral pattern, the irregular pieces growing smaller as the pattern drew inward, culminating in a center rectangle of black satin embroidered with a bunch of wildflowers. My eyes went right to that visual destination. Though various embroidery stitches connected all the edges of the pieces, only the center one was ornamented within, except for one mysterious little wheat sheaf partway down toward the right corner. The entire assemblage flowed together in anything but a "crazy" fashion, as though this woman who had created it, consciously or not, had winnowed down visually, though descending stages, to what mattered: that center piece with its loving elaboration of stitchery. She had led me to the core. It was a beautifully judged summation, with the pieces—no more, no less—contributing to her vision. This quilt presented a world of its own.

I have studied my photographs many times, also revisited the quilt itself. But the lingering impression, as though my mind had adopted the quilt and its arrangement—call it an intuited vision of possibility—has been with me ever since. Just as this unknown woman had created this masterpiece, the vision suggested that I, too, could bring many different pieces together, just in a book.

I have wondered since if these pieces were all she had; I doubt it. Also, I am sure she did not translate each one into a piece of her life's existence, expressing significance—I made that translation. I feel sure, however, that she exercised great selectivity as well as artistry; that she cut and cut again, pieced and re-pieced, tried various layouts, and sought out both visual echoes and a balance between bright and dark colors. The arrangement is carefully considered yet does not appear rigid; at

the same time, this is the work of a
strong woman who knows what she
wants and who will persist until she
gets it. Someone who knows herself.

How much farther could such
"translative" spirit-to-spirit thinking
get from the Buffingtons and
their Red Notebook recordings of
cottage repairs? (Though I learned
that I also possess similar abilities
and found myself drawing on them
many times in the years to come.)

My response to the quilt,
claiming it as having something to do with my own writing, was just
one—though a dominant one—of a wildly mixed set of inspirations
that have kept me going. I can describe myself as a multimedia
influenced writer. The practical Buffingtons might well find my
impressionistic approach, even my desire to write, problematic and
even, well, "crazy."

Not surprisingly, the book—and my confidence—grew slowly and in
bursts. One inspiration was a favorite English novel, Barbara Pym's *Jane
and Prudence*. In my journal, I noted a letter Jane writes to Prudence,
describing the country village where she and her husband have settled:
"Such richness here!" In her elegant London apartment, Prudence
reads this claim with astonishment, no doubt wondering how on earth
Jane finds "richness" in a provincial place. I went on to note, *However
temporarily, I reside in the village of Buffington, the Buffington demesne,
one might say.*

Both asserting territory and skulking around imaginatively, I
worked to notice every detail of Craigville. As a Pym afficionado,
and also a fan of personal memoir, letters, and diaries, I had long
been fascinated by domestic life—and here I was being served up

a particularly rich slice. *Keep watching and noticing, Sally! Don't let anything get by you.*

One morning a couple of summers later, I awoke from an arresting dream, one of the kind I have learned to recognize as *Pay attention, Sally* messages from my mind. In this one, I had been involved with rehearsals of a play in the style of Arthur Miller. Costumed in a bright yellow jersey dress, my character both dominated and charged the dramatic action. After one scene near the end of the dream, I said to the others performing with me, "That's amazing, it's so *strong* I can hardly manage it!"

A bright yellow dress? On waking, I immediately remembered the enlarged portrait of Mom and Dad on the mantel, in which Mom wore just such a garment. That attention-grabbing color animates the picture and creates a perfect background for her beloved Leica on its strap around her neck.

I was taking Mom's part. Taking on her famous strength and force— as well as her position of photographer. My inner self was surprised at what I had found myself doing, yet I had gotten up my guts and stepped forward. Now I was the one doing something important, the one with the vision. The one who would speak for the cottage.

Around the table in the dining room: Andy and I, Pete, my friend Ellen from California, and our old Massachusetts friends, Carl and Kathy. A brilliant red tablecloth and lighted candles reflected the glow of our happy, sunned faces.

As she does in any gathering, Kathy sparkled: loquacious and fun, laughing a lot, she was throwing out ideas all over the place. With enthusiasm! Carl and Ellen looked grave, though their eyes followed all the opinions and exclamations bouncing around. From Dad's old place at the far end of the table, Pete's mustached visage looked toward me; to my right, Andy talked and laughed as he passed plates and poured wine. I had served a good dinner, too: scallops, fresh green beans, and potato salad, all washed down with cold Sauvignon Blanc, plus for dessert, several kinds of ice cream and hot fudge sauce. No wonder my journal entry later described this as a "chatty evening."

Earlier I had announced that once we were finished, I planned to read aloud some of my writing. *I used to join Andy and Carl in making music, but words are what I perform these days.*

As I started on *Afoot*, I noticed Carl looking apprehensive. *Maybe this kind of thing is somehow threatening to him? Or is it just a major change in how he knows me?* Next to him, Kathy leaned toward me with a smile of intense interest; Ellen knitted her brow, and I sensed Pete seriously considering every word.

I read well, making sure to look up and make eye contact, and left pauses where needed.

After my serious declarations in *Afoot*, however, I could see that they needed a break. *Good, they're enjoying this next one!* Kathy in particular, as she was a great cook and had met up with the same situation I had written of—how to use up summer cottage leftovers—though I doubt that she had ever thought of invoking Thoreau in that connection.

When I finished, I was thoroughly congratulated, though I was surprised when Kathy said, "Oh, I could never have done that! You're so brave!"

Hmm? "Brave?" This from a self-made woman who's taught school for thirty years and who exudes confidence 24/7?. . . Well, I guess sharing the product of your thinking and work is something else again . . . . I'm proud that I've done it, though, and I thank God for the spirit I feel.

Later Andy complimented me with great warmth. *Wow! I'm so happy.* For both on past musical occasions and now with writing, my performing had been a problem between us. From our early days together, I had found Andy's intense, no-holds-barred style of critique tough indeed; slowly, we had managed to forge some ground rules about discussing my work, but such a wholehearted compliment was rare and high praise indeed. After all, I was writing about Craigville, his family's place, right on their very home hearth.

Maybe I am brave.

By this time, however, I had been putting writing out in public for a good fifteen years. Experience in musical performance had stood me in good stead; I knew how to act confident whether I felt it or not, how to relate to an audience, not to apologize, how to dress, and above all, to be prepared. Yet writing came with far more on-the-spot criticism than music ever had. Attending summer writing workshops around the country, I had read to lots of strangers and endured some disparaging evaluations. I had published work, too, essays on music and several poems.

Still, a Buffington audience—now that was something else again. A home crowd situation that reminded me of Jesus being a "prophet without honor in his own land" (Mark 6:4). Reading that evening, however, had been no sudden decision; I had been feeling a growing confidence, a need to put myself out there.

Oh, confidence! Having enough faith in your work to stand up on a stage or read to the family or submit manuscripts for publication. Confidence means being sure of having something to say, something you consider valuable or unique or funny. Confidence that the product of your mind, your thinking, your voice, is needed by other people: Listen to *me*! I am worth your attention.

Another piece of self-definition. Journal entry. "Little pocket of time. A shaft of light slants in and creates a wide pair of stripes across my page. As the pen bobs across the paper, my shadowing hand creates a moving display. The bursts of bluey purple statice in the vase are intensified by solar highlight, and the non-writing end of my pen also traps light, casting little dashes of sun on the desk objects as I write." Then a rough tracing of my writing/right hand, done by my left. Grandly I inscribed the (very) rough sketch, "The Writer's Hand."

I also made a wonderful and generous friend in the village of Craigville, Valerie Lane, who has taken deep interest in my writing. Every summer she reunited with several writing friends, and in 2013 I was invited to join them for a potluck gathering. George Comeaux read a few newspaper pieces he had written and a poem about the Red Sox; Valerie read parts of a children's book based on stories her father had told her. When it came my turn, I once again selected *Afoot*, feeling that it was my strongest work to date. As I read, I realized anew how serious a piece it was.

Though I came away unsure how well I had fitted in, the group invited me back the next summer and again gave me generous attention. We sat out by the marsh and watched the sunset, sipping wine on the deck. This time, I read shorter pieces about the cottage, one on cooking and another about weather. They asked about my plans for the book. I journaled later, "I can honestly say that they 'hung on my every word.'" George told me, "If you ever do an audio book or it's suggested that you have one, don't let anyone else read it!"

Oh, that comment pleased me! *I have a voice, whether I speak out loud or on paper.*

Another summer, however, I found myself speaking out on quite a different occasion. For decades, management of the conference center in the village of Craigville had been carried out by the Massachusetts Conference of the United Church of Christ, an arrangement set up decades before by Andy's father and others, building on the village's religious campground beginnings. However, in 2014 the conference gave notice that it wished to withdraw. Of course, this was the hot button issue of the summer.

Late in August, a public meeting was held. Conference representatives restated their position, then opened the meeting for questions and comments. In generally polite, though strained, tones, local residents made statements. Most of the opinions expressed devolved into "Oh, you can't go!" or "We've always done it this way, Craigville needs the conference. You can't let us down!"

I raised my hand.

"I'm Sally Buffington, and I'm here because I married into Craigville. That was almost fifty years ago now." A ripple of laughter. "I'm sad this step is being contemplated, after all the history, but I also know that the Massachusetts Conference is having financial problems these days, as are other UCC conferences around the country. So perhaps we need to think of their side of the issue. I'm sure the conference doesn't wish to take this step but feels it must."

The conference minister looked at me gratefully.

"I wish, though, that the conference could give Craigville management more wiggle room. May I suggest a couple of years' delay, so that the village isn't cast off so abruptly? I think that would make a great difference to planning for the future. In any event, I wish the conference well with all the challenges."

A few more speakers, then the meeting ended; on schedule, the conference went ahead with its action. Since then, the Craigville Conference Center has found new management and continued successfully.

What I said was not important; what was, that I spoke up when Andy and Pete did not. I could not help wondering if they were following their father's dictum: "You don't have to explain anything you didn't say." Yet to this day, I feel that one or the other should have stood up for, or at least publicly evoked and honored, Dad's foundational work and purposes.

Instead, his daughter-in-law was the only Buffington to speak.

One more dream. This time, the situation was that I would conduct a woodwind group, ten or so young musicians playing together for the first time, and train them into a solid ensemble. As they all sat down, with music for a dozen pieces on their stands, one young man asked, "Which ones will we perform in the concert?"

"I'll make the selection after we read them all through; once I see our strengths, then I'll choose what goes best."

I asked for a tuning note. "Play a concert C, which will sound as B flat."

Raising my arms and hands, I signaled the musicians to play, then hold the B flat. "Keep holding this note, take a breath whenever you need it, but keep coming back in, keep playing." As the pitch continued, it magically swelled into multiple voices—all ranges, high, middle, and low—a great, deep, resonant B flat chord! I realized it was the invocation chord of the great Mozart *Serenade for Thirteen Winds*.

Then I awoke.

Yet the chord kept sounding and resounding within me. I hear it now as I write.

I was bringing disparate things and different voices together: I knew each pitch and sound, then the unified whole. The chord was a signal that someday I would know—I would feel sure—how to bring together all the necessary elements of my book into a harmonious, balanced arrangement. The chord was my voice, all those sounds and stories within me, thought and lived, blended into words: a reverberant signal not to give up.

But several more notes of the chord remained to be played before I could live fully in the cottage and know my role—know myself. Sounding and expressing that inner voice, was still no easy matter, though my confidence was growing. For me to speak fully, out loud, more work lay ahead, yet my hopes were real and reachable. As long as I kept holding on and breathing life into them.

TRACING THE PATHS

"**O**h, good, now we're getting there! Straight through this light, then we should see the church just up ahead." *Turns out to be farther away than I had thought . . . . Strange, all these twists and turns and signs to watch for, to get to a place of quiet, private exploration.*

Finally, however, I spotted the sign for St. David's Church. "Here it is!"

Turning in, seeing signs with arrows pointing to the labyrinth, we drove toward the back of the premises, beyond several weathered-shingle buildings. *Hmm, this is rather the way our cottage is placed, too: part of a community, yet somewhat separate and next to the woods.*

An ancient spiritual practice, a labyrinth is a visible, tangible mandala which can be placed indoors or out. At first glance, its outline suggests a ripple pattern in a pool, but the paths within lead you all over: across, around, and back and forth.

Rather than a maze designed to confuse, a labyrinth is a framework for meditation that you engage through walking. Thoughts and ideas spring to mind with each step, and often after you have finished. Anything but a simple "into the center and then back out" pattern, at times walking a labyrinth feels as though you are meandering—yet you are also part of something unfolding.

I had brought friends along, Kathy and Ellen. The three of us were welcomed by a profusion of hydrangeas blossoming on the church grounds—pink, bluey-lavender, and creamy white. Sun shone on the circle forty feet across with a base of compacted gray sand and paths outlined in red brick. At that moment, the labyrinth looked like a vast flower with a petaled bloom at its center, as though the earth had offered up something beautiful—a way to make sense of life.

Kathy started first, and a few moments later, Ellen. After taking several deep breaths, I, too, started in and took several steps straight ahead, then was led onto a curving path to the left. Now a U turn, after which I turned left once more and walked back along a parallel arc. I found myself tracing paths near yet not at the center. *It always seems like you're getting there right away . . . yet you're held back for a while . . . rather like when I came to the cottage in the early years. I physically reached the place but sometimes felt on the outside looking in.*

One foot, other foot. On I went. I had stepped out of everyday life to carry out a reflective practice, all the while doing ordinary things like breathing, walking, and thinking. Minus, however, keys, ID, purse—and a list, that tool I so frequently use. *I bet Mom made lists! . . . She was so organized. And she had to be, keeping that cottage going . . . . Did she ever walk a labyrinth, I wonder?*

Though the labyrinth is not a series of concentric circles, many of its paths run in parallel arcs. I found myself close to, but not touching Ellen; I could see Kathy over on the far side, making her way around one of the longest arcs. Her wavy hair was blowing and framing her open expression and gray eyes. Later we came face to face and embraced before moving along on our respective paths. *What a generous, warm-hearted friend!*

One foot, other foot. One foot, other foot. I was progressing at *Andante*, a walking tempo for music. I kept going, thankful for the sense that there are no mistakes when you walk the labyrinth. The easy physical motion frees your thoughts, too. *Did Mom like me? I wasn't always sure . . . . It's been years now since she died, and I'm still trying to understand our relationship.*

Glancing around, I saw that Ellen had reached the center. Arms folded, almost clasped around her body, she appeared drawn into herself. I knew she had heavy matters on her mind. The labyrinth was a wonderful way for us to share without the need for moment-by-moment conversation. *I hope this walk today will help her . . . really that her whole stay with us will, though I'm unsure what she needs most.*

Eventually, I, too, reached the center and stood stretching for several moments, eyes closed, happy to feel the sun. I felt as though I had reached a destination, yet knew I was only halfway.

Life at the cottage had been a happy sequence of taking care of friends and family, cooking, photography, and writing. I had also been reviewing what I had written about Mom. *Am I being fair? Should I have made those judgments? . . . You've been beating yourself up a lot, Sally, worrying that you shouldn't judge Mom or feel guilty about learning by acting contrary to her ways. Don't! We all learn things however we can, and this is typical of the younger generation making its way. It's all right to do that, even natural.*

Now I began the second half of the labyrinth. Ellen was moving slowly; Kathy had reached another quadrant far ahead. As so often happens, it felt as though the paths themselves were moving us. I loved the sense of being part of a great plan, yet not feeling controlled or driven.

So often in the cottage we all just reacted to Mom. She was the center, so were we all bodies that spun in orbit around her? . . . That setup worked for a long time, but she sure became defensive and difficult those last years . . . . How many times—hundreds of thousands, probably—did Mom and I both walk our paths? Circling the kitchen, in and around the house, up and down the stairs, inside and out.

Step by step. Step by step. I had not been moving quickly yet found myself headed out the exit path, as though I were coming down the path from the cottage to the road. I had taken the same straight way in, made it to the center—the heart—and then headed back out, cleared and re-set. Renewed.

Ellen stood waiting over near some trees, with an air of resolve. Kathy sat on nearby steps, her back to the sun, looking up at the sky. We all smiled at each other with a sense of silent communion. Nobody had tried to change anybody, no one had tried to dictate the other's steps or direction. *I wish Mom and I had been able to view our time together in the cottage more like that labyrinth walk. I suppose we went the same direction but at different speeds and in different patterns . . . . Maybe it is time for me to simply forgive Mom. To acknowledge that things were tough on us both, that she was who she was—like me. Probably we did as well as we could have, two ordinary women who found it hard to share territory.*

I thought again about my two friends. They balanced each other and took turns. Ellen, self-contained and thoughtful, and in her ebullience, Kathy rather like Mom. But I felt her equal. *Was it just generational, that I couldn't ever feel that I was Mom's equal?*

At the cottage, Mom was in charge—and very much the extrovert. When I grew bolder and asserted myself, I think Mom found me threatening. *But I respect her, sort of . . . . I even wonder now if I have grown into loving Mom because she has caused me to wonder so much, to try to understand her? And through this, I've been forced—or stimulated, a happier word—to better understand myself.*

Back in the car, none of us said much for a while. *Perhaps all the talk, the endless volubility of the family in the cottage, was one reason Mom and I found ourselves in a maze rather than a labyrinth. The Buffington style is what I think of as public, informational talk . . . . Mom and I wandered into different ways of doing and being and came to impasses. All too often we walked without enough respect for each other's path.*

Kathy, Ellen, and I had taken a journey to a place of journeying, driven paths leading to and from the labyrinth—and once we had walked, as though the roads themselves propelled us, we returned to our weathered old cottage, went up the path to the front door, and walked in.

Later, as I so often have, I thought of Rilke's famous words: ". . . be patient toward all that is unsolved in your heart . . . and try to love the questions themselves."

I thought of the visual pattern of the labyrinth. The whole beautiful clustered set of curving paths might stand for the upper rounded part of a question mark and as I walked, I was the human dot that completed the symbol. The labyrinth had helped me formulate questions or rearrange them in my mind, yet I was necessary for it to function. By extension, I was conceiving of life itself as walking, always questioning and puzzling over my experiences as I went.

Rilke goes on, "Perhaps you will . . . live along some distant day into the answer." A hopeful point of view. But I notice the word "perhaps." Perhaps I never will never figure out this relationship with Mom, never learn the answer, or answers.

Why do I keep at this? All these years after Mom died, when so much has changed and time has moved on, do I indulge in fussy, self-justifying agonizing? I still feel I somehow failed with her, this challenging but intriguing woman with so much to teach me and to delight in knowing. I wonder what I could have done better.

How did I wish Mom's and my relationship had been different?

Surely, some of those times we clashed, my distress was obvious, but I do not recall Mom ever apologizing. Nothing ever got talked over or solved. She was forceful enough that to initiate any dialogue was daunting. In conversation, she often made a big deal about children not getting their way via tantrums, a view I agree with—but isn't an adult blowing up and then ignoring the issues and never changing anything pretty much the equivalent? I had to just keep guessing, make some of the same mistakes again, or maybe change just enough that I improved matters by pure chance.

So another of my questions, a very difficult one to "love" in Rilke's term, is this: what if you are left angry and there is no resolution? And you learn nothing that will help you avoid these times in future. Perhaps this is when a labyrinth becomes a maze and you are confronted with a dead end.

Probably I will never find any single answer or anything more than contributing reasons or the generational or in-law conflict. I realize, too, perhaps I am attempting to force Mom into walking a pattern that would never have worked for her. Perhaps she did not know what to do or to make of me, or what steps to take.

For my part, for the years I have kept the cottage going, I have come to act by a kind of creed. I want the cottage to be a place where there are no dead ends. May it be instead a place where we all walk freely and work out ways to share the paths when we find the going difficult.

I believe there is no one way to live here. Or to walk. Or be. Though perhaps one person oversees beds, kitchen, and meals, etc., anyone who comes can make his or her own decisions. I hope to make it so everyone is accommodated, feels accepted, and can relax. Enjoy this great place! We touch, use, and share the same rooms and dishes and beds, gaze on the same beloved views, talk and share experience, but no one feels it the same way or is expected to.

Come with friends or family members or alone. Stay for a long or short time. Float through your stay or live your summer days tackling questions and ideas. Your impressions will be different from those of the people with you. That's fine. Walk wherever you wish over and over, visit again and again. The paths await you, in this sometimes festive, sometimes meditative place, this house of steps and journeys that is Craigville.

CLOSING

*L*ast day for the summer. Andy and I lug our suitcases out onto the front step, then check the windows and doors "one more once." The light next to the door has been taken down and stashed safely away, as have the old rotating doorbells in their wrought iron frame. The barbecue has been exiled to the garage and the porch bench taken in, too. The place is stripped.

Down we go to the cellar. Time to haul up the slab of unpainted, grayed plywood which replaces the screen door we've been using all summer. I hold the slab in place while Andy drops rusted pins in the hinges and latches two hooks on the other side. Now the inner front door, with its handsome panel of Judy's stained glass, is completely obscured.

"Oh, I just hate that thing! It looks so ugly! And you know, any determined vandal could just unlatch it and break the glass or one of the windows. It'd be a cinch to get in here!"

"But it's a barrier," Andy says. "You know, it says KEEP OUT. That's why we do it. It's a deterrent if someone comes around looking for trouble."

Stepping back a few paces, I take a picture: slab door, white frame, empty house. Then I turn and snap the view of the marsh, a far happier memory to take home. As often happens the day we leave, the marsh could not possibly look fresher, the water bluer, or the reeds greener as they sway in the breeze.

We have put the lid on the coffin of summer.

Yet it is time to go. I'm tired. Tired of being away from home, tired of Buffingtons, tired of Craigville. These last few days, I have sometimes felt as though I never would get home.

Also, the air has turned chill and windy. Dried-up brown leaves scraped and swirled across the road as I drove in yesterday. The village is melancholy and largely emptied out and, at night, everything is dark indeed.

As for the closing process, probably none of us, if left on our own, would just lock the door and go off leaving everything in place for the whole winter. We'd strip the beds, do laundry, clean out the refrigerator, and clear the shelves; take in outdoor furniture, lock the doors, also drag in the Astroturf carpet from the porch. Call the plumber to turn off the water. Shut off electricity. Basic stuff.

But would I do these things? "Spread moss flakes on rug." Carry "glass–toped [sic] table from porch upstairs and store in Joanna's room." Lug the Norman Brumm owl picture "to lg. upstairs bedroom." Would I join others in hefting the porch settee "to bedroom over kitchen"?

No! Why lug furniture upstairs? I have not the faintest idea what moss flakes are, either. I, too, treasure the owl picture, but why stash it anywhere but the living room where it hangs?

We are not, however, left to our own devices to close: we have The List, whose four single-spaced pages Mom composed and typed up years ago. However, thanks to Andy's edit in 2005, it got reduced by half. Still, we check off items. "Plastic bag stuffed animals, leave in center bedroom." "Drape TV with sheet." "Clotheslines and fold-up drying rack into cellar." "Ceremonial ax and African masks go to bedroom closet." "Cover maritime oil picture with newspaper or dish towels from kitchen, and also the two bookcase spines (living room) to slow fading." Further admonitions: "Vacuum all rugs, lock all windows, doors, cover all lampshades with plastic bags (keeps out most dust), large pictures in beds between box springs and mattresses." I wonder if we will find spider webs over or inside the lampshades, now that we no longer drape every single lamp in a plastic bag, a concession I argued for.

The list keeps getting revised, though. Recently, by a vote of three to one, we decided to no longer stash framed pictures between mattresses and box springs; instead, they will be stored in drawers or stacked against walls, a change due in part to Dean's tale. "You know, Memorial Day weekend, when Jo and I opened the house last spring, I woke up the first morning and something felt funny about the bed—and what do you know? There was still a picture under the mattress! Thank God the glass didn't break!"

One exception, however: Mom's big needlepointed Persian scene, her masterpiece, is still to be stored between a mattress and box spring to protect its woolen threads from moths, albeit with a note of warning left for next year's opener. We also extend no hospitality to any varmints or creatures. The chimneys have long been capped to prevent coons nesting. The list goes on. "All candles into boxes. . . seal tightly, mice eat candles." They also eat cornmeal and cardboard containers, as I found out the hard way. Soap gets sealed up, too, and as I press the plastic lid down on a box of bars of Irish Spring, I picture a bunch of disgusted mice muttering, "Well, let's go, boys. Nuttin' to eat here, not even a measly chip in the shower stall! Stingy bastards, these Buffingtons." The last day, we pull the kitchen table out from the wall and stack counter drawers on it at angles (the list terms this "pigpen style") and always we "shut the pantry door to keep out mice."

All this care of possessions—there must be a fine line indeed between reasonable caution and way-beyond-necessary fussing. So much of the process is a matter of opinion, anyway.

And what of the famous Biblical passage? "Lay not up for yourselves treasures upon earth, where moth and rust doth corrupt, and where thieves break through and steal, but lay up for yourselves treasures in heaven . . . for where your treasure is, there will your heart be also" (Matthew 6:19-21). Perhaps all this closing business is hoarding thinly disguised as prudence and wise management.

No. More is at stake here; the list is a way to organize a process. For our hearts are in that cottage; it *is* our treasure. So closing involves such matters as loyalty, family, and even mortality.

For years, I never participated in closing. Much as young people do
not think much about death or how to deal with it, I had the luxury
of ignoring the whole business. Also, with children, the start of school
meant we had to fly home before Labor Day. Only much later did I
become an adult in the full lifecycle of the cottage.

My first experience of closing, though, in 2005, set me on edge.
All that damned housework, one of my least favorite things. I did not
behave well. Who wants to vacuum, pack away, and lift heavy stuff?
Who likes making a house less comfortable or dismantling familiar
arrangements? Who wants to dodge around upstairs, bending and
maneuvering to clean, when the view is gorgeous out on the porch
and you can sit with a cup of coffee or tea and gaze at the marsh? It all
amounts to a purposeful destruction of an enjoyed status quo. Closing
is like digging a hole, burying yourself, and pulling the sand in over
your head.

Since then, I have helped with closing several times and have gotten
better at handling my emotions, but I still find it hard. For one thing,
closing always stirs in me a sense of obligation: make an assessment,
Sally. No one tests or rates me, yet sometime in the last few days of my
stay, I think *How did I do this year?* I have recorded such self-judgments
as ". . . no very original cooking, nothing memorable on my part . . . .
The place has been draggy and less vital this summer . . . . This house
needs spark—new interest and young people. I am getting more and
more pessimistic as to how we will keep it going . . . ."

Closing loads our last days with responsibility; closing also grinds
in the inexorable change of seasons. At home in California, I no longer
think of fall as a sign that winter is coming. Though many people
would say this makes for a bland and contrast-less existence, to me it
spells optimism and the expectation that I will keep enjoying life.

Another reason closing has become such a job is that we have made
things complicated. For instance, a couple of summers ago, Andy,
Pete, and I bought the cottage a record player. Yes, a phonograph.
For a long time, I had noticed those dusty stacks of LPs, also two

long shelves of old 78 rpm records in albums: folk songs recorded by Richard Dyer Bennett, and Marais and Miranda, plus album after album of symphonies and concertos. Would anyone ever play them? We discussed giving them away.

However, once we'd bought the record player, Pete and Andy sorted first the LPs (easier to handle) and next the 78s. Then we listened to Dyer Bennett, Marais and Miranda, and also to an impossibly perfect mariachi band, and to the British comedy team of Flanders and Swann. More than once, I thought, *Oh, so that's where that old catch phrase came from!* Andy would hand Pete an album. "Oh, I remember that one!"—and out would come a story or memory of when they first heard the music, or the verses or lines they liked most.

The records were yet another way to hang onto the old days. Even when we changed or railed at some thing or custom from the past, we were taking note of it. Respecting it. I came to think, *In this cottage, people never really die.* When for the twentieth time we marveled at how Dad could lie directly on sand and sleep facedown, he was still with us, alive in our evoked image. When I told Andy how shocked Mom would have been at my throwing away a bag of odds and ends after cleaning out the fridge for the last time, I was acknowledging that her pronouncements and attitudes still rang in my ears—even if I did not always follow them.

With every summer, the place becomes ever more a family homestead; also, I remind myself that Mom used to come here and live for a well-equipped entire summer. I have aided and abetted the process, too. Look at the candles! Look at the pretty table settings and flowers and pottery pieces! Because there is a homemaker in me at work here, too.

Down at the end of the closing list comes the more public stuff. Pete takes the porch flags down and folds them away, and I take in the *Buffington* sign and stash it in the garage so that no one can expect to find us home anymore. Andy and Pete take on the Walkabout section: "Check for things not put away, missed screens, whatever . . . ." An important detail: "Bring in the outside key."

Also, "File Change of Address forms at post office."

Recently a Craigville family we have known for years changed their address for good. By chance, I happened by their cottage just as their real estate agent matter-of-factly took down the For Sale sign.

Margot, whom I like immensely, was soldiering away at vacating. Feeling awful. "Selling's the rational thing to do," she told me, "but it's the hardest thing I've ever done." However, with rising insurance rates, taxes, and needed upkeep of the cottage, holding on had come to be too much. Like us, Margot and her family live at a distance, though not so far away as California.

She gestured toward a table piled with stuff awaiting Goodwill pick-up. "Take anything you want, but I bet you've got all in this your cottage, too!" True.

Trying to be helpful, I selected some Post-it notes, paper clips, and a blue homespun tablecloth with matching napkins. Margot warned, "It's probably stained, Sally!"

"I don't care. I've had dinner on it here, I'm sure!"

I wanted the cloth to remind me of their cottage, which is one of the coziest places I have ever known. A nest. I loved visiting there, especially the charming kitchen with open shelves displaying the eclectic equipment of gifted cooks. I asked Margot after her parents, who have been dear friends to us all for so long. "Oh, they're in their nineties and still going strong!" Her mother Sue is a wonderful hostess, as is Margot herself. Lively, intelligent, and fun, they always made me feel at home, feel liked. Often an evening there featured "rough croquet" out back by the marsh, a giggly game on soggy, hillocky grass. I remember dinners and parties, leaf-filtered sunlight in late afternoons, torrents of good talk and laughter, someone's cute dog being passed from hug to hug, and lots of gin and tonics or cold white wine.

Memories rushed to my mind like delicious tastes, along with the bitterness of ending. A beloved place gone, enjoyed by a family for over seventy years. A place much like ours: a house with soul. *Will we, too, have to close for good someday?*

Joking, I have called our cottage an ark because it is such a boxy, old, wooden place, though you could never call our minor hillside

Mount anything, let alone Mount Ararat. But perhaps the water is going down around us; maybe Craigville as our Buffington center, will be left high and dry. Do family summer places have their time—and then come to an end?

I am on my way upstairs one evening about 6:30 when a patch of light catches my eye. Channeled through a window and the open front door, setting sun has struck varnished wood and created a patch that looks like a polished specimen of tiger's eye, a horizontal oblong perhaps eight by twenty inches. A shaft from the west, kindled by solar fire millions of miles away, the patch blazes on an old oak closet door in the upstairs hall. Pausing on the step just below the second floor, I watch it glow, almost pulsate with light. The wood grain stands out, like stripes on the surface. Then the light begins to fade and, with the slowly sinking sun, all the surrounding surfaces darken into shadow. And the ember disappears back into its wooden hearth.

Over the years, I have come to think of closing as stuffing the house into a winter cocoon, with the happy idea that our haven will then burst forth again in spring. Yet, though I am generally an optimist, there is also something darker present. Once, as I draped old sheets and plastic drop cloths over the beds upstairs, I caught myself thinking of them as shrouds. Emily Dickinson's words sprang to mind. "The bustle in a house, the morning after death . . ." Always now, I sense shadows lurking, like dark gray-black shifting shapes that slither along the floor or leak out from behind me or materialize before my eyes, only to vanish a second later. But I know they will pop up again.

As inevitably, as quietly as a leaf or pine needle falling, closing warns me that some day at the cottage will be my last. *Someday this will end.*

When the door closes after me then, I wonder if I will know.

Over the winter, I often picture the cottage, closed and empty, sitting on its hill above the marsh. Through wind and rain, storms and snow, the cottage prevails; the old shingles weather, their basic gray taking on streaks of green and brown. Winter bleaches the grass into pale hair-like strands and all around, tired old brown oak leaves carpet the ground, revealing the bare branches above. Perching like a dowdy old hen, feathers gathered around her, the cottage holds our place. It is not really closed, I tell myself, just sleeping. Waiting for us to return and awaken it, waiting for our next year of summer. And spring will come and refresh the lawn and trees. Green will seep back in, and foliage will clothe the branches once more. The days will lengthen; and as spring turns to summer, we will come again.

LAST DAY

*T*he gray overcast sky hardly lifted my mood, but no other weather would have done any better. Andy's and my suitcases stood packed by the door. For the last several weeks, we had been engaged in a million jobs. Having done everything we could think of, we were worn out; and Jim Lane, the kind friend who would take us to the bus station, was to arrive in twenty minutes.

September 4, 2019. Andy and I were closing Craigville for the last time.

As the cottage was being sold furnished, the rooms were down to basics. Bed, chair, bureau, and night table; or couch, end table, chairs, and coffee table. A magazine or two remained, here and there a few framed pictures still dotted the walls, plus the old native ax above the door to the downstairs bedroom, that odd travel relic that seemed to belong to the place. No one had wanted to take it. And the kitchen? Someone could move right in and cook there, though with only one guide at hand (a duplicate *Joy of Cooking*) rather than the former three-shelf culinary library. The obedient old gray pans stood waiting, the cast iron frying pans hung from their hooks. But in all, the place looked and felt about as stripped as I could imagine while still meriting the term "furnished."

Leaving Andy to whatever private fussing he still wanted to do, I fled out the front door and across the lawn. About to turn onto the path in the woods, I caught sight of a pair of swans and four cygnets swimming in the river. *Oh, no, a swan song* . . . . I paused, then took a final image of the twisted tree sculpture I had come to love, two spiraling arm-thickness trunks that together suggested a dancer.

As I slouched my way over the hillside, the loamy dirt yielded underfoot. *This is the last time I walk this path as my own ground . . . the last time I can check in on that fat trunk flexing its arm, the last time I can inspect those weathered trees . . . the puzzle pieces of bark strewn about and the silvering chunks of wood, all the lines in their grain . . . and those holes* . . . . *My last chance to see what strange mushrooms have popped up overnight and to wonder whose teeth have been nibbling the edges.*

Coming out by the old garden-clippings pile, I was delighted to find a thriving patch of Indian pipe. I took one last long look at the bend in the river, where the clumps of marsh grass looked like mussed hair in need of combing.

A spot of cheer: a brilliant red trident-shaped tupelo leaf that seemed to say, "Christmas is coming!" Now I passed the back steps and the wasp nest I had worried about; thank goodness the creatures had kept to themselves all summer, in their big gray helmet-like house right above the back door.

Once more across the flat side of the path below the dining room, then up to the front door, where I came upon Jim and Andy, ready to go.

Oh, no. This is it. I stood there with a lump in my throat. I felt almost unable to move, even to breathe.

We are really going. Leaving this dear old place. How I wish I could condense all these years into this spot right now and relive them all. But I have to go.

"Oh, this is awful . . . . But we've got to make the bus! Here, Jim, let me manage that big bag there—I'm sure it's overweight."

The three of us wrestled the luggage out. Andy paused before going down the path. "You sure we've got everything?" He meant our travel documents—and the entire wave of emotional baggage we were taking along.

"Yup. Got the bus tickets right here in my purse, in this big envelope, and the flight information is with them."

He pulled the front door shut.

Thud.

I took one last look at the porch and the lump rose again in my throat. Then I turned and shouldered my handbag and maneuvered the heavy suitcase down the path, working to keep it from dragging me.

And we drove away and left Craigville behind.

Though I will return to Cape Cod and visit the village of Craigville, I will never again live there. Our turn is done. Our cottage will change, as it must for the new owners to make it theirs and take it to their hearts. As their ownership begins, I wish them joy and years of warm memories.

I wonder if they will ever feel me as a ghost, the way I felt Mom's spirit in the cottage. At first, taking her seat at the dining room table felt like plumping down in her lap. More recently it has also felt strange indeed to take over her preferred reading chair, though I didn't use the little old cast iron footstool she liked.

Now I will walk my paths in the house only in memory: from kitchen to porch, upstairs and down, from pantry to stove, dish in hand, or from the kitchen to the table or silverware drawer. Surely some remnant of me will forever hover over the sink, and over that sweet spot of counter by the window. That is, until someone remodels the kitchen, which it could use. Surely some body-ghoulie will always groan in the upstairs bedrooms under the sloping gables; I will not miss making those beds and all that bending and twisting around bedposts.

Then there are the paths I have trodden into the floorboards, the invisible but indelible wear, the neatly piled sheets and pillowcases, and unseen thousands of my fingerprints on doorknobs and house keys. My footprints have joined all the others on the front porch planks, especially my morning route out the front door, then out over the front lawn to the overlook on the marsh.

All these paths, all these layers, were like sheets of mica on a rock, the transparent, incremental degrees by which I grew into the place, every moment of every day I lived there. Each peeled-off sheet represents another way I earned, I adored, my way in.

Or did the cottage itself use them to seep into me?

It has worked on me through Andy. Through the deep good fortune of our more than five decades of marriage, I have shared and grown sideways into his memories, stories which took on greater reality as we slept in the bedroom he has always slept in, or when I shivered with him as we got up on a chilly morning like the one when the family came down long ago, in early spring or late fall. The memories seeped in deeper, grew more real with every telling—and now I am in my seventies, I understand those cottage happenings even better.

In turn, Andy and I have replicated Dad's and Mom's experiences, as I thought one dark early September evening as we sat at the dining table together. Too chilly for the porch, we agreed, but the house loomed dark and empty around us. Now we two were the older generation holding the fort, keeping going.

For Craigville had come down to Andy and me. After several years of increasing mental decline, our dear Pete was no longer on hand, instead residing in a memory-care institution. Sadly, this had made the job of leaving far easier—and bestowed mercy on Pete himself. He so loved the cottage, loved every scrap of family history: every possession, precious or dime-store, every glass and saucer and teacup. He loved every clipping or out-of-date business card or out-of-print book or faded snapshot or gewgaw or running trophy or tourist brochure. Every piece of tarnished silver came with a memory attached. Leaving and packing up with him, even at his best, would have been a nightmare. For him, and for us.

Also, as so often happens in families, Craigville was largely Andy's and mine; for the next generation, our daughters and niece, either could not or did not wish to take over the cottage.

We all felt a terrible wrench. Yet we agreed, it was time. Andy was more than ready to give up the worry of maintaining a hundred-year-old house; so was Joanna. We carried out the transfer without rancor, and in an organized manner. I think we acted much as Robert Frost put it: "to bow with a grace to reason/and accept the end of a love or a season."

And still the process and loss have ground on us both.

When we left that final day, we both knew that while we might come back to visit, never again would this cottage be *our place*. This pinpoint on planet earth that we knew so well would turn into a house lived in only in memory, only in thinking back. No longer in steps taken or nights slept, nor coffee pots filled nor morning sightings. No more family suppers on the porch. No longer would we put the key in the lock and step into "Old friend house."

Thankful for the long-held privilege of coming there at all, we honored this gift of good fortune with a vast amount of work and respect. We gave ourselves to the cottage, for an increasingly major portion of our year; we kept it alive and shared it with many people. It has taken continued loyalty and spirit. And I am proud of what we have done, both in owning and in leaving.

THE TENT WITHIN

A few nights before we were to leave, I awoke at three in the morning, my right leg seized up with a cramp. *Oh, I was so comfy—until this! And we've been pushing so hard closing up these last few days. I don't want to get up . . . . Come on, walk it off, Sally.* I heaved up my unwilling body.

Soon, though, as I paced the creaky old floors and my leg relaxed back into its normal state, I began to enjoy myself. Looking out from the bedroom across the hall, our neighbors' blue-white bug zapper glowed supernaturally, and I could trace shafts of light across the wrinkled surface of the water, coming from cottages across the marsh.

Now I walked to the other side, pausing at the window of the guest bedroom. Below me, a streetlamp cast an eerie atmosphere. *This view is like one of those old N. C. Wyeth illustrations, maybe for* Treasure Island. *Has our respectable neighborhood become the setting for some skullduggery? . . . Maybe I'll witness a secret rendezvous, hidden figures skulking about or masked desperados . . . . The asphalt looks almost white . . . . And who's lurking in the shadows behind those tall spruces?*

Of course, no such things were going on. But as I stood there watching the old houses looming around us, the pointed tips and rounded clumps of trees, and remembering the dark bulk within which I stood, I thought, *I'm not just the only one awake right now, I'm the only one who's really present. Alive and breathing in this place on earth at this moment . . . . But that's an illusion, isn't it? . . . It's like saying I own this view or this house . . . . For this half-light vision won't last—and very soon, memory will furnish my only hold.*

After a while, cramp long gone and fatigue reasserting itself, I padded back into our room. Hanging up my robe, I crawled into bed and contoured up next to Andy. Wow, that was grand . . . . *Oh, I am going to miss this place.*

Another vision, this time from far above. About ten years before the night I have just described, Andy and I traveled to Nantucket, one of the two islands south of Cape Cod. On a sparkling clear October day, we left Boston and were flying down along the south shore of Massachusetts, when out the window in the distance, Cape Cod came into view, looking so tiny and vulnerable I felt a rush of protective love. *Only a sandy little strand . . . it seems to just float out there . . . looks as though solid ground doesn't go down very far at all.*

Flying farther south, the landmass became more substantial, though much of the land looked (as I knew it was) downright porous. All those blue spots, like holes in a sponge, were the kettle ponds, tidal inlets, and marshes of Cape Cod.

"Oh, there's Sandy Neck!" And more prosaic local landmarks. "There's the water tower in Centerville . . . and Lake Elizabeth!"

On to the twists and turns of the Centerville River, our marsh, and the village of Craigville: the whole place spread out like a map. Almost immediately we came on the crescent curve of Craigville Beach; the rows of old gray bath houses looked like stubby fingers.

But where was Craigville? Here I was expecting to personally Google our great old cottage from the sky—and I couldn't see it. The cottage was invisible. Nestled—no, completely concealed—in trees and foliage. Like Peter Pan's Neverland hideout, you had to know how to find it.

Much of the time I view Craigville from a vast distance; I mentally stroll around and through the cottage doing exactly as I please. I am freer, one might even say, safer this way; no one can disagree with me or get in my way as I think, review photographs, or write what I wish from the other coast. Yet I have felt that same freedom on the east coast, too. All these years of going to Craigville, and all my labor has created that world for me. Or have I created its world for myself?

A house cannot cause you to do things, cannot compel you to action. Yet as I have lived there, it has come to seem that the house makes things happen. I think of the old saying, "Your home is your castle." Your place of hold on the earth, your stamp of self-definition, if you will. I am also reminded of Mark Doty's words, "When you love a place enough, it seems almost to be inside you, as if it were the physical equivalent of an inner life."

Even on those brief early visits, I lived both within the cottage and within myself. Like the tent Thoreau used in the woods before he built his cabin, I carried with me temporary shelter I could pitch any time I wanted. In time my tent morphed into the cottage itself, having now become a frame that, in Thoreau's words, "reacted upon the builder." And as Craigville came to supply or suggest all I needed, I was inspired to develop my own voice.

However, certainly never on that first winter visit so long ago, nor during most of my returns east, did I think, *This place is going to mark me*. I just went there and did what I thought daughters-in-law were supposed to do. Come the summer of 2000, however, given my newly free circumstances, Craigville took on an almost formal identity which I now think of in that old-fashioned term for a school: a temple of learning. In that odd second adolescence, that mature-yet-I'm-growing-up-again season, the cottage became simultaneously my campus, teacher, and laboratory for ideas. In the process, instead of the idealistic Walden-like concept of Cape Cod I'd grown up with, Henry Beston's *Outermost House*, I found myself an innermost house in a very populated place, also a rather odd one. Not only was our house built out of another building, a creative recycling, but it had also become a container for possessions and a place of extraordinary richness almost haphazardly achieved—and a composite portrait of its family.

I find myself looking back now with a sort of *Our Town* view. Both of Thornton Wilder's famous lines are true: "Oh, earth, you're too wonderful for anybody to realize you" and "My, wasn't life awful–and wonderful." The place got crowded: too many people, the generations rubbing on one another or someone treading on someone else's territory, those humid August days when everyone was irritable and growly. The product of all these pieces and more, yet Craigville achieved a mixed beauty, even sweetness, those nights on the porch when soft descending rays of golden light covered us all.

Perhaps it is no wonder that seeing the so-called crazy quilt at our neighbors' house awakened my nascent idea of a cottage memoir. This place could be expressed only in disparate pieces brought together with some kind of rangy but discerning overview, with an outsider's way of looking at it all.

I am that outsider. I love the place, even as I have acted as an agent of change. I have given myself to Craigville, often in varying degrees, often with difficulty—and with whole-bodied delight, as I did one August evening.

Everyone else had turned in. The day had been humid and sticky and, though we had kept every window open, warm air was still trapped inside. About ten o'clock, I went out on the front lawn and looked around. *Oh, it's so cool and lovely out here! I am so tired of everything sticking to me, clothes and upholstery . . . Every surface is damp, even wood, too, when you've sat a long time . . . . I wish I could just take off my clothes . . . . Well, why not? I don't think anyone will see.*

But my bare feet reminded me this was hardly the softest grass, studded as it was with twigs and the occasional pinecone; I might need something to lie on. I went back in for a towel, then spread it on a patch of ground among the trees. Looking around, I saw no one, so peeled off my clothes and lay down naked in the dark.

Among the leaves and grass, the softest, lightest fabric of breeze brushed all over my skin. I felt myself relax, and my body spread a little as I took breath after quiet, deep breath. I heard distant voices, the chirp of crickets; the night rustled and stirred. I let myself dream, as though I were floating on this ground. *I have immersed myself in this place, almost blended into it . . . . I am part of Craigville.* My eyes followed the gently swaying web of branches. I spotted stars in the spaces between, winking in and out as the lines moved . . . . *I am completely here now . . . baring myself. I am making a clean breast of me, with no barriers, no "in" or "out." Just me, here. Open to this place on earth, this generous ground for living. This place I love.*

As our days dwindled down, I asked myself over and over, *How can I leave? Leave this windy center of earth? Leave behind what is offered here . . . this scene, this place I have stepped into, where I feel and notice and breathe and think and write.*

Everything was full of mystery and holiness, and I had been given this place to perceive, to write into being mine. All of it part of this family cottage and its land that I had never known before I met Andy. Craigville took me in and molded me, and within it, I have built my own Cape Cod house.

ACKNOWLEDGMENTS

As a child, I regarded authors as heroic individuals who braved whatever the world threw at them to Write A Book. Or books. However, I have long since realized that while the writer's vision propels the whole process, almost no one—certainly not I—achieves a book without help and encouragement from other people. Looking back now, this book seems more than ever to be an *E pluribus unum* production. So I would like to thank the many people who have helped me along the way and who have supported my vision of the cottage at Craigville.

First of all, for the book you hold in your hands: Jeniffer Thompson of Monkey C Media. Jeniffer, I felt the current of your enthusiasm from the day we met. You have helped me to fly and I've drawn such support and inspiration from your professional work. I also thank the staff at Monkey C Media, especially Chad Thompson, Kat Endries, Ella Gregory, and Julio Pompa.

I have received immense editorial guidance and coaching from Diane Lefer, Marni Freedman, Karla Olson, and Andrea Glass. Laurie Gibson and Lynette Smith have guided me so many ways in preparing the manuscript. I am deeply grateful to all of you.

I would like also to pay tribute to two of my early writing teachers, Rick Geist and Marc Nieson.

232 | S.ALLY W. BUFFINGTON

A major vote of thanks to my beta readers, Rhonda Kendle and Terry Weiner. You worked so hard for me and your detailed suggestions improved the book greatly.

For over twenty years, I've been privileged to be a member of a writing group with Mary Graham, Sharon Reynolds, and Sue Zolliker. A toast to you guys! And thank you for critique, for friendship, your patience with my successive versions, and all the just plain fun we have had together.

A particular thanks to some women who I consider The Friends of This Book: above all, Charlene Reichert and Sharon Reynolds. While the word "support" is often over-used, it applies here; you two have stuck with me and my writing all the way. Ellen Cook, Kathy Douglas, Paula Elizabeth, and Valerie Lane are also friends of *A Place Like This*.

In addition, I thank Gina Abelkop, Alice Brown, Anne Buffington, Joanna Buffington, Katherine Buffington, George Comeaux, Lucia Galloway Dick, Iona Dickinson, Ann Donner, Margot Fisher, Ann Forcier, Tom Frenkel, Betsey Hanson, Joanne Hartunian, Laurie Higgins, Helen Jacobs, Cindy Jenson-Elliott, Meridith Lafrenz, Sue Lederhouse, Gerry May, Mary McDermott, Lisa Movius, Ross Putnam, Helen Reichert, Linda Sieh, John Watson, Kelley Worrall, Loretta Worters, and Carol Yeager. A special round of applause to Linda Sommer and thanks to the members of her book group, who listened to early versions of some chapters.

I am grateful to Ed and Patricia Deyton for the vision of the crazy quilt in their possession.

At the heart of *A Place Like This* is my husband Andy. There is no way to thank him enough.

This book is in memory of my beloved father, Bill Woodworth, and his brother, my dear Uncle Fran.

DISCUSSION QUESTIONS

1. What is "a Cape Cod cottage"? The idea and its connotations are deeply important to Sally.

2. Why does Sally cling to this vision throughout her life? Does some kind of Cape Cod mystique exist? What is it?

3. Theodore Roosevelt once wrote, referring to his Long Island home, "I wonder if you will ever know how much I love Sagamore Hill." How does a summer cottage or *escape place* come to matter so deeply to people? Such a place is often a sign of wealth or privilege. Can it be deserved or shared?

4. Describing herself when she was about to marry into the Buffington family, Sally wrote, "No one else regarded the world quite the way I did." Did she change over the years, or remain fundamentally the same person?

5. How does Sally's concept of family and relationships change as she lives through the years of visiting Craigville? Can an in-law (mother or father) influence the next generation as profoundly as a birth parent?

6. Sally's encounters with Lois Buffington reflect changes in women's lives in the twentieth century. Do you think Lois could have found a way to use her professional training?

7. How did life at the cottage highlight the choices Lois and Sally had made?

8. Food and cooking are pretty important at Craigville. But what if you don't like blueberry pie?

9. Or, consider the time and work such a pie requires? How do a cook's work and style influence daily life around her or him? How would you describe Sally's style?

10. In *One Old Chair*, Sally says, ". . . if you had taken a picture, you knew something. You had taken command of the situation." Why does she feel that way? Why was photography so important to her at Craigville?

11. Sally writes of nature as her "escape from all these human complications into a world I conceive entirely in my own terms." Is that all she finds there? What do you find in the natural world? Do you have to be alone to experience it?

12. Why does it take Sally so long to write the book and gain the confidence to present herself?

Publisher's Note: Sally is available for book clubs and interviews. For more information, please visit her website at SallyBuffington.com.

ABOUT THE AUTHOR

Sally Buffington is a writer and photographer, also a classically trained musician. From her home in southern California, she migrates back to native ground in Massachusetts, especially her spiritual homeland of Cape Cod. Writing lyrically and imaginatively, ever aware of sensory experience and memory, Buffington takes the reader into her thoughts wherever she finds herself.

Follow Sally on social:

Facebook: /SallyBuffingtonAuthor
Instagram: @SallyBuffingtonAuthor